Factoring Wisdom: A Preview of Buying Receivables

Short Sayings and Straight Talk for New & Small Factors

Jeff Callender

DASH POINT PUBLISHING

Federal Way, Washington

Factoring Wisdom:
A Preview of Buying Receivables
Short Sayings and Straight Talk
for New & Small Factors
by Jeff Callender

Published by:
Dash Point Publishing, Inc.
P.O. Box 25591
Federal Way, WA 98093-2591 U.S.A.

Website: www.DashPointPublishing.com

©2003, 2005 (1st edition); 2012 (2nd edition)

This publication is designed to provide accurate and authoritative information in regard to the subject mattered covered. It is sold with the understanding that the author and publisher are not engaged in rendering professional services. If professional advice or other expert assistance is required, the services of a competent professional person should be sought.

While every reasonable attempt has been made to obtain accurate information, the author and publisher hereby disclaim any liability for problems due to errors, omissions, or changed information in this publication.

Fictitious names of people and companies are used in this book. Any similarity between these and names of actual people and companies is unintended and purely coincidental.

Library of Congress Control Number: 2012943553

ISBN: 978-1-938837-00-5 (Paperback)
ISBN: 978-1-938837-12-8 (PDF)
ISBN: 978-1-938837-18-0 (Kindle)
ISBN: 978-1-938837-06-7 (ePub)

Printed in the United States of America.

Dedication

To My Family

Contents

Preface

I have always enjoyed reading books of collected sayings of my favorite authors. So after writing several books and ebooks, all of which focused on the subject of factoring accounts receivable, the idea of creating this collection seemed like a good way to introduce the principles and practices of factoring. Here, these concepts are presented in very small doses anyone can understand, learn from, and enjoy.

This book is a collection of selected short quotes. These maxims give a brief summary of practical advice and simple sayings you can use in your factoring business – whether you are just starting as a broker, have a few small clients of your own, or fund a portfolio of clients totaling millions of dollars.

These quotes are listed alphabetically by topic. Because some touch on two or three subjects, you'll find a few included under more than one topic. This just underscores that particular saying's importance.

Many of these axioms reflect sections or even the entire chapter of the book from which they come, yet are condensed to one or a few sentences. By reading these you will get a thumbnail sketch of the contents and educational value of the other material, which will hopefully kindle your interest in the subject and lead you to learn more. Thus, this is the first book in The Small Factor Series.

Just like a movie trailer gives a taste of what a film is about, this book encourages you to see the whole picture revealed in the other volumes. I hope you read *Factoring Wisdom: A Preview of Buying Receivables* both before and after reading the other books and ebooks quoted here. Using this volume as bookends to the others, you will gain a good grasp and understanding of what factoring is all about – and what being a factor is really like.

Jeff Callender

Factoring Wisdom

Note

Sources that follow the quotations include the name of the book or resource in italics, followed by the name of the chapter or subsection in which the quote is found.

+ + +

ACH Transfers

ACH stands for Automated Clearing House and is also known as EFT, for Electronic Funds Transfer, and direct deposit. You can send ACH's through your bank (if it provides them; once again some smaller banks and credit unions do not) or through an ACH service. ACH payments are a very handy way of making deposits to your clients.

How to Run a Small Factoring Business
Banking and Funds Transfers

ACH is an electronic transfer using the bank's money. These transfers are made through the Federal Reserve Bank and go directly from your bank to your client's bank. That means you're transferring money with no float and the transfer of funds is immediate. You could transfer funds you don't have in your account, and disappear the next day. Therefore the bank looks upon this daily transfer as a loan for which you must qualify.

How to Run a Small Factoring Business
Additional Resources: A True Story about ACH Transfers and Bankers

If you decide you want to transfer funds with ACH – which will save a lot of time – come armed with a very strong balance sheet and a lot of liquidity.

How to Run a Small Factoring Business
Additional Resources: A True Story about ACH Transfers and Bankers

Accounts Payable Departments

Despite often Herculean efforts on your part to provide a Notice of Assignment and make follow up calls to be sure they will pay you and not the client, followed by assurances they will, guess what? Many customers *still* make their checks to your clients anyway. This leads you to wonder about the intelligence of a great many accounts payable departments across the country, as well as being one of the most effective means of rapidly turning your hair gray.

How to Run a Small Factoring Business
Banking and Funds Transfers

While an NOA can be correctly executed at the beginning – properly delivered, properly received, properly noted by the customer's Accounts Payable department – it can take no time, a little time or quite some time for that same AP department to really mess it up.

Top 10 Illusions about Risk and Loss
#7: Once a Customer Receives a Notice of Assignment, Sending Payment to the Factor as Instructed Will Not Be a Problem

Despite all these steps, I never cease to be amazed how frequently payment over notice occurs. Dealing with AP departments for many years has led me to develop a kind of conspiracy theory against factors.

How to Run a Small Factoring Business
Record Keeping

Advances

Make it your policy not to advance on any invoice until the work is finished and is signed off by the customer or can be verified. Period. Make this clear from the very beginning so your client never even thinks to ask in the first place... though he very likely will ask anyway just to test you. Kind of like your kids.

How to Run a Small Factoring Business
Common Mistakes

Advantages of Factoring as a Business

You stock nothing, manufacture nothing, sell no product, and have no raw materials to replenish. You provide a service with a universally needed commodity: cash. Because that's stored in your bank account, it doesn't take any room in your garage.

Fundamentals for Factors
Is Factoring Right for You?

If your family is a good team and each person understands his or her role, as well as the others' roles, you can enjoy working this business for quite some time.

Fundamentals for Factors
Is Factoring Right for You?

Application Process

If you have ever applied for a bank loan, you'll find the application process with factors to be much simpler and faster.

Factoring: Sell Your Invoices Today, Get Cash Tomorrow
Signing On

Bad Debt

If a prospect wants to factor poor paying customers who are nothing more than bad debts, she doesn't understand what factoring can really do, and is better off contacting a collection agency. Factors want to buy good receivables, not bad debt.

Fundamentals for Factors
Risk Management Tools

Factors are not collection companies who thrive on deadbeat payers. Factors are financiers who invest in dependable payments coming from solid companies. They do not want to purchase bad debt.

Factoring: Sell Your Invoices Today, Get Cash Tomorrow
Faulty Assumptions and Mistakes to Avoid

There's only one good thing about receiving a client's bankruptcy court notice: you're usually not surprised when you receive it. The bad thing is, you can just about count on writing off whatever you're owed as a bad debt.

Top 10 Statements You Never Want to Hear
#8: "Notice of Chapter 7 [or 11 or 13] Bankruptcy Case"

Classic avoidance tactics are not returning phone calls, giving you the runaround, promising payments that never materialize, saying a payment is in the mail when it is not, and too often as a final straw, having the phone number disconnected. The bankruptcy notice, when it arrives, is the frosting on the cake. All you have to do now is eat it (so to speak).

Top 10 Statements You Never Want to Hear
#8: "Notice of Chapter 7 [or 11 or 13] Bankruptcy Case"

Bad Debt Reserves

Each time an invoice is paid, set aside a percentage of that income into a Bad Debt Reserve account. Put these dollars into a savings or other interest bearing account that is separate from your regular operating account. Consistently add to it so it will always be there to ease the sting if you ever experience a loss.

Fundamentals for Factors
Risk Management Tools

Banks

I am the first to recommend companies who can get a bank loan or line of credit at a very good rate to do so. It's cheaper money, plain and simple. But what do you do when banks won't even talk to you in the first place? What do you do when you've tapped your line and the bank won't extend it, or won't provide a new loan? What do you do when your bank calls your loan or pulls your line of credit? Is factoring "too expensive" then? This is the situation in which many small business owners find themselves.

Top 10 Misconceptions about Factoring
#3: Factoring Is Too Expensive

When a business simply *cannot* obtain a bank loan or line, an SBA loan, venture capital, or angel investors, factoring is usually the *only* form of funding available.

Factoring: Sell Your Invoices Today, Get Cash Tomorrow
Why Haven't I Heard of This Before?

When clients come to you, remember that most arrive with their self-esteem bruised and battered by bank rejections. So be gentle with them. Do your best to help them. If you can factor their receivables, routinely provide excellent service. If you do, you will appear to be riding in on a white horse and will have their utter loyalty.
How to Run a Small Factoring Business
Additional Resources: ACH and a Story about Bankers

As a factor needing regular cooperation from your bank, you must understand how banks work. Financial ratios can mean more than your history, especially with large banks in which decisions are made by people far removed from your friendly local branch. And even more, a good word from the right person can change a decision that might otherwise go against you.
How to Run a Small Factoring Business
Additional Resources: A True Story about ACH Transfers and Bankers

The bigger issue to the bank, apparently, was the fact that I was a factor – which some banks consider a high-risk industry. This made me a high-risk customer in their eyes despite my perfect record. They didn't want me sending "their" money to clients of any size. The higher ups at the bank were clearly most concerned with risk control, not my good record or needs as a customer.
How to Run a Small Factoring Business
Additional Resources: A True Story about ACH Transfers and Bankers

Benefits of Factoring

If using these services (billing, A/R collections follow-up, credit screening, and so on) enables you to eliminate these tasks from in-house staff, you'll lower your expenses and/or give your staff other responsibilities. This can improve your profit margin in addition to increasing sales. Therefore you need to consider not only the costs of factoring, but the benefits as well.
Factoring: Sell Your Invoices Today, Get Cash Tomorrow
Faulty Assumptions and Mistakes to Avoid

The whole point of factoring your receivables is to help your company. When used correctly, factoring can certainly do this. After working in this industry for two decades, I still marvel at what an incredible financial tool factoring is.

Top 10 Questions to Ask When Looking for a Factor
#1: "Is This Actually Going to Help My Company?"

Boredom

While procedures need to be followed, factoring is anything but boring.

Fundamentals for Factors
Is Factoring Right for You?

If you find this boring you need to take up extreme sports for a living.

Fundamentals for Factors
Is Factoring Right for You?

Brokering

Factor small deals, refer big ones.

How to Run a Small Factoring Business
Bits of Wisdom for the Small Factor

Set an absolute ceiling which no client's credit limit will exceed. If a client outgrows this limit, broker him to a larger factor and continue to earn commissions, or participate with another factor and share the income (and risk).

Factoring Case Studies (2nd Edition)
Assessment

Broker Agreement

Always have a formal agreement in place with any funder *prior* to sending a prospect for evaluation. If you don't, you can lose many, many thousands of dollars on a deal.

Factoring Case Studies, 2nd edition
Smuggley, Swindol, & Finkbottom Finance

Be very careful to whom you send any deals, especially large ones. Even with written agreements in place, I've heard horror stories from brokers who said they had referred deals to factors or funders – and had a signed Broker Agreement – who a short time later unilaterally decided the broker just wasn't going to get paid. They knew if the broker (almost always a very small company) tried to sue, they had far more legal resources than the broker and could simply starve the broker out. The broker wouldn't be able to afford a court battle, even if the unpaid commissions were sizeable.

Factoring Case Studies, 2nd edition
Smuggley, Swindol, & Finkbottom Finance

Not all factors and funders have high ethical standards. With any referral, be sure you are dealing with a company with integrity, and get it in writing.

Factoring Case Studies, 2nd edition
Smuggley, Swindol, & Finkbottom Finance

Brokers

A good broker can save you a great deal of effort and searching, and be a tremendous help locating, then evaluating, which factor may be best suited for you. While a broker will not know every charge and procedure of every factor, he will know which factors serve your size company, industry, region, and other preliminary considerations. This knowledge will save you the time of eliminating many factors that aren't a match for your company in these regards. His experience in the industry can help steer you toward good factors (and away from not so good ones), and make your decision easier and faster.

Top 10 Questions to Ask When Looking for a Factor
#2: "Adding It Up: What Does This Really Cost?"

Experienced, good brokers will recommend a single factor based on your needs. If you find that factor doesn't work, the broker can then refer another. Good brokers won't give you the names of four or five factors to start, as the factors referred will quickly realize the account is being "shopped" and not be interested because of their upfront due diligence costs.

Top 10 Questions to Ask When Looking for a Factor
#2: "Adding It Up: What Does This Really Cost?"

A good broker is a valuable asset to the industry, for both the business owner seeking a factor, and the factor seeking new clients. With a good broker (who should not cost the client anything) the business owner knows he's saving a lot of time and is being referred to good factor. The factor knows he's getting a prequalified referral who should meet his parameters.

Top 10 Questions to Ask When Looking for a Factor
#2: "Adding It Up: What Does This Really Cost?"

For the business owner seeking a factor, a talented broker will match you with the factor best suited to your particular business and needs. The broker's knowledge and contacts can save the client countless hours of what could prove to be a frustrating search, particularly if the business owner is new to factoring and has no idea where to look or what to look for.

Factoring: Sell Your Invoices Today, Get Cash Tomorrow
How to Find a Factor

A phone call from a good broker who has brought valuable business in the past is always a welcome event to any factor, and will be greeted with exceptional interest.

Factoring: Sell Your Invoices Today, Get Cash Tomorrow
How to Find a Factor

Factoring small invoices with very small companies is the best way to learn first-hand what factoring involves and requires. By being a factor for small accounts, you'll be a much better broker for big ones.

How to Run a Small Factoring Business
Bits of Wisdom for the Small Factor

Caution

You need to keep up your guard for every account you have, new and long-standing. With every client you need to do exactly what the factor did here: "proceed with caution."

Factoring Case Studies, 2nd edition
Hemisphere and World Logistics International Transfer (HAWLIT)

Clients in Financial Crisis

A craving for cash followed by dishonest and deceptive acts cloud their reason, extinguish their common sense, and make them do very foolish things.

How to Run a Small Factoring Business
Common Mistakes

When a client is in dire straits, the unfortunate fact is this: you, his factor, are usually the very last person he tells.
Top 10 Statements You Never Want to Hear
#2: "I Needed the Money"

First, the client will tell himself you are a "rich factor" who has plenty of money (or at least more than he has), and you can "afford" the loss but he cannot. Second, when he is in this frame of mind, you and the money you are owed are of secondary importance to him. His own survival is far more important than what happens to you or anyone else.
Top 10 Statements You Never Want to Hear
#2: "I Needed the Money"

Clients' actions are based on perceived self-interest, especially if they are in financial trouble. In other words, a client will do what he thinks is best for him, especially if he's desperate...and everyone else can go hang.
Top 10 Statements You Never Want to Hear
#2: "I Needed the Money"

Clients, Bad

Always remember this maxim: **no client is better than a bad client**. The longer you factor the more you'll realize how true this is.
How to Run a Small Factoring Business
24 Common Mistakes

While having no clients provides you with no income, having no clients also doesn't result in a loss of your funds, sleep, sense of well-being, and healthy blood pressure.
Top 10 Insights about Factoring Prospects
#1: Having No Client Is Better Than Having a Bad Client

When asking yourself if this is a quality investment, also ask: "Which do I want: no client or a bad client?"
Top 10 Insights about Factoring Prospects
#1: Having No Client Is Better Than Having a Bad Client

Some might assume that a good client is one that makes you money and wonder, "If an account is making you money, can that still be a bad client?" The answer is a simple "yes."

Top 10 Insights about Factoring Prospects
#1: Having No Client Is Better Than Having a Bad Client

I have had clients who have given me an education in how NOT to run a business. Those are the clients who want to bend the rules, who cop payment checks and see nothing wrong with it, or who bounce from one crisis to another like the steel ball in a pinball machine. Such people are just not on top of running their business, let alone keeping track of their receivables.

How to Run a Small Factoring Business
Additional Resources: The Secret to Getting Paid

You simply *never* know which new clients will be good experiences, and which will be bad.

Factoring Case Studies, 2nd edition
Hemisphere and World Logistics International Transfer (HAWLIT)

Clients, Dishonest

Especially during your learning and beginning period, you may take a hit or two because of the "Newbie" tattoo etched on your forehead for all to see, especially clients. A few of them will not be honest and try to capitalize on your greenhorn status.

How I Run My One-Person Factoring Business
Key Points

Less experienced and often very small factors who are used to trusting people are usually shocked the first time a client is not only dishonest, but acts defensive about what he's done, and certainly acts less than grateful for the factor's help.

Top 10 Illusions about Risk and Loss
#10: When You Provide Money for Clients and Help Their Businesses, in Return You Can Expect Them to Always Be Grateful and Honest with You

Nearly every factor has had the experience of a client who's in a bind and contacts the customer with "new" instructions for the customer:

pay him directly. This is of course fraud, but too seldom will that stop a client from pulling this one.

Top 10 Illusions about Risk and Loss
#7: Once a Customer Receives a Notice of Assignment, Sending Payment to the Factor as Instructed Will Not Be a Problem

It dawned on me something fishy was going on and I suddenly had the sick feeling my star client was taking me for a ride. As a factor, this is one of those realizations that literally can make you feel like you're going to throw up.

Factoring Case Studies, 2nd edition
Mr. Scumbucket Janitorial Company

Never underestimate the nerve of dishonest clients. I had one temp agency client forge every time card she submitted for months.

How to Run a Small Factoring Business
Record Keeping

Despite the fact that he had clearly defrauded me and I was out quite a bit of money because of his actions, he wanted to know when he would be getting his rebate and escrow reserve returned!

Factoring Case Studies, 2nd edition
Hardluck Harvey's Homes

As Harvey's fraud extended over time, he became harder and harder to reach. Again, this is a classic, extremely common move by someone who has done something dishonest. The less they have contact with you, the harder it is for you to pin them down and find out what really happened. Factors usually end up getting the truth from almost anyone *except* the dishonest client.

Factoring Case Studies, 2nd edition
Hardluck Harvey's Homes

Clients, Good

Ask any experienced factor this question: "What are the types of clients you most prefer?" and most will answer, "The ones I've had for a long time."

Top 10 Illusions about Risk and Loss
#1: There Is Little or No Risk Posed By a Client =Who Has Factored with You for Years

You're looking for people who are basically good, honest, hard-working folks who play by the rules.

Top 10 Insights about Factoring Prospects
#5: What Does My Due Diligence Tell Me about This Individual's Personal Character?

As you work through your underwriting you will be continually asking the question, "What does my due diligence tell me about this individual's personal character?" If, overall, it shows you someone who is honest, works hard and is a good risk, then this person may indeed become a good client.

Top 10 Insights about Factoring Prospects
#5: What Does My Due Diligence Tell Me about This Individual's Personal Character?

Clients who receive factored checks just too easily deposit them, either in ignorance or in silence. Having a client who actually does the right thing – sending the checks to you – is the way it should be, but much too often isn't.

Factoring Case Studies, 2ⁿᵈ edition
Onin's Workouts & Isometric Exercise Systems (OWIES)

You simply never know which new clients will be good experiences, and which will be bad.

Factoring Case Studies, 2ⁿᵈ edition
Hemisphere and World Logistics International Transfer (HAWLIT)

This is a client I will never forget, both because he was such a good client for so long, as well as for the anguish he put me through just trying to collect a debt he acknowledged he owed – by agreeing to two different workouts. You just never know which clients are going to be bad or good. You also don't know which good clients are going to stay that way.

Factoring Case Studies, 2ⁿᵈ edition
Mr. Scumbucket Janitorial Company

Clients, Prospective

Good prospective clients are those who have business-to-business and/or business-to-government invoices, and who wait approximately two weeks to two months to receive payment.
Fundamentals for Factors
Identifying and Locating Prospective Clients

To help recognize good prospective clients, ask yourself these questions:
- To whom do they sell?
- How long do they wait for payment?
- Will they benefit from immediate cash advances?

Fundamentals for Factors
Identifying and Locating Prospective Clients

First and foremost clients need to be honest people with integrity. If you get the sense they might do something shady with any business transactions, chances are high you will be one of their first targets.
Fundamentals for Factors
Risk Management Tools

If you get a bite from a prospect who ends up making you nervous, let him go and put your line back in the water. For some reason, interested prospects tend to come in waves, and you may well get another bite quickly from someone who could be a far better catch.
How to Run a Small Factoring Business
Common Mistakes

Most factors who have accepted new clients as a favor to someone usually end up regretting the decision.
How to Run a Small Factoring Business
Common Mistakes

When considering a new prospect, one of the very first questions you always need to ask is "Do I Want to Buy the Invoices to This Prospect's Customers?" Having a clear answer to this question for each prospect will make your decision to approve or decline a prospect much easier.
Top 10 Insights about Factoring Prospects
#7: Do I Want to Buy the Invoices to This Prospect's Customers?

One of your jobs when considering prospective clients is to take everything into account and try to create a picture in your mind of the question, "What can go wrong with this deal?"
Top 10 Insights about Factoring Prospects
#3: What Can Go Wrong With This Deal?

Being a good factor or good factoring broker means you recognize the prospect's real needs, and can point him or her to someone who will provide the best solution. When you're considering a new prospect, consider what their real "itch" is, and whether factoring provides the right "scratch."
Top 10 Insights about Factoring Prospects
#10: What Is This Person's Itch, and Will Factoring Provide the Right Scratch?

Select your clients very carefully and don't take on anyone who will not pay you back. That's kind of like Will Rogers' advice for investing in the stock market: "Buy some good stock, and hold it till it goes up, then sell it. If it don't go up, don't buy it."
Top 10 Illusions about Risk and Loss
#3: You Have a Very Good Chance of Recovering Lost Funds by Retaining a Collection Agency or Attorney

Paraphrased version of Will Rogers' quote for factors: "Take on some good clients who won't rip you off, buy their invoices, and make good money. If they rip you off, don't accept them as a client."
Top 10 Illusions about Risk and Loss
#3: You Have a Very Good Chance of Recovering Lost Funds by Retaining a Collection Agency or Attorney

Clients, Religious

Sometimes I hear factors say they're more wary of people who appear to be quite religious than people who are not religious at all. Other factors have less trust for people of no religious persuasion. My thinking tends to fall somewhere in the middle. The spiritual leanings of factoring clients – either highly religious or absolutely not religious at all – come in at absolute zero as an accurate means of predicting which clients will be honest and full of integrity, and which ones will stab you in the back the first chance they get.

Top 10 Illusions about Risk and Loss
#8: There Is Less Risk Factoring People with Strong Religious Beliefs

I have learned the hard way that just because someone "talks the talk" and has every appearance of being a person of deep religious convictions, that *doesn't* mean two things:
1) it doesn't mean they're telling you the truth, or
2) it doesn't mean they won't lie to you or pull a fast one, all the while draped in sanctimonious language and pious pretentions.

Top 10 Illusions about Risk and Loss
#8: There Is Less Risk Factoring People with Strong Religious Beliefs

The religious leanings of a client have absolutely nothing to do with the potential risk they pose, with their propensity for honesty, and with their inclination (or lack of it) to do what's right, especially if it means they'll lose money.

Top 10 Illusions about Risk and Loss
#8: There Is Less Risk Factoring People with Strong Religious Beliefs

I have worked with numerous church people over the years who wear their faith on their sleeves, "talk the talk," and go out of their way to make clear they have been saved. Unfortunately, when push comes to shove, in many cases, the need for money overcomes the desire to do the right thing and they have left me holding the bag – if not outright defrauded me.

Factoring Case Studies, 2nd edition
Dee Seetful and Associates

I have worked with very unreligious people who were more honest and trustworthy than other clients who were quite involved in their church and active in their faith. I've also dealt with very religious people who have shown admirable honesty and integrity when it meant taking it on the chin, far more so than other clients who were of no religious bent. In short, it just really doesn't matter.

Top 10 Illusions about Risk and Loss
#8: There Is Less Risk Factoring People with Strong Religious Beliefs

The lesson here? Don't assume anything about any clients, especially when they talk about (or don't talk about) their faith. *Anyone* is capable of *anything*.

Top 10 Illusions about Risk and Loss
#8: There Is Less Risk Factoring People with Strong Religious Beliefs

Clients, Small

If given the choice, I'd take ten very small, low maintenance clients over one bigger client with erratic dependability, questionable quality of work, and lack of integrity, any time.

Factoring Case Studies, 2nd edition
Smallnhappy Graphic Arts

Personally, I like working with little guys. They suit me just fine. I also like the idea of never paying five figures in legal fees.

How to Run a Small Factoring Business
Additional Resources: A Small Factor's Thoughts about Big Factors' Concerns

Clients' Uniqueness

No two clients or customers are alike, even in the same industry. Each business and business owner are unique, and exposure to them will provide a never-ending parade of interesting people and ventures right before your eyes.

Fundamentals for Factors
Is Factoring Right for You?

Collection Agencies

A factor, rather than being a collection agency, is an investor in good receivables – not bad debt. The last thing a factor wants to buy is an account that will take a lot of time and effort to collect.

Top 10 Misconceptions about Factoring
#8: "You Should Factor Your Slowest Paying and Deadbeat Customers"; Alternate: "Factors Are Like Collection Agencies"

Sometimes people mistakenly think factors are collection agencies. Be quite clear: they are not. Collection agencies exist to collect payment from problem accounts and deadbeats who have skipped out on paying legitimate bills. Not only are factors *not* collection agencies, most actually use the services of collection agencies and collection attorneys themselves when they realize they have a problem account.

Top 10 Misconceptions about Factoring
#8: "You Should Factor Your Slowest Paying and Deadbeat Customers"; Alternate: "Factors Are Like Collection Agencies"

One may wonder if there is any way at all for a factor to recover lost funds. Well of course there is, and the method for recovering these funds may well be the world's *second* oldest profession: the collection agency.

Top 10 Illusions about Risk and Loss
#3: You Have a Very Good Chance of Recovering Lost Funds by Retaining a Collection Agency or Attorney

Give late payers to collections sooner rather than later.

Top 10 Statements You Never Want to Hear
#4: "Don't Worry…You'll Get Your Money Back"

The moment you think an account is a problem, give it to collections. Don't wait and hem and haw; the longer you wait the harder it is to collect, and the more the collection agency will keep if they collect anything.

Top 10 Illusions about Risk and Loss
#3: You Have a Very Good Chance of Recovering Lost Funds by Retaining a Collection Agency or Attorney

When a problem account is given to collections, one of the first things the collection agency or attorney asks is, "Do you have a signed Personal Guarantee?"

Top 10 Illusions about Risk and Loss
#5: The Signature on Your Contract or Personal Guarantee of a Different Person than the One Receiving Advances Provides You Adequate Legal Protection

Collection agencies who tell you their recovery percentage will speak glowingly of collecting 30 or 35% of funds. That means that, on the average, for every $1,000 you give to a collection agency, you may collect some or all of it a third of the time – not that they will collect $300 every time you give them $1000 to collect.

Top 10 Illusions about Risk and Loss
#3: You Have a Very Good Chance of Recovering Lost Funds by Retaining a Collection Agency or Attorney

Collections

The most unpleasant aspect of factoring, to my thinking, is trying to collect from clients or customers who have become unresponsive and elusive.

How to Run a Small Factoring Business
Additional Resources: A Small Factor's Thoughts about Big Factors' Concerns

Sad to say, when it comes to getting paid being nice is often ineffective. Not that you have to be mean to get paid; just persistent and consistent.

How to Run a Small Factoring Business
Additional Resources: The Secret to Getting Paid

Comfortable

Don't ever get too comfortable with the paper or the people. That doesn't mean that you should act like the money police necessarily, but it is wise to always trust but verify. In this case, this client became a "friend." It was because of that "friendship" that I told my little voice to hush, that everything would be fine.

Factoring Case Studies, 2nd edition
Clank Brothers Wiring and Cable

Common Sense

I never cease to be amazed at how little common sense some new factors use when they start.

Fundamentals for Factors
Risk Management Tools

Numerous risks go with factoring – dishonest, selfish, careless, and otherwise untrustworthy clients and customers, and errors in procedures or judgment made by factors. Therefore common sense suggests a factor's foremost strategy is to set financial limits, thereby putting minimal amounts at risk. This is especially prudent when the factor is new, even if his or her pool of factoring funds is sizeable.
Factoring Case Studies (2nd Edition)
Assessment

Common sense doesn't cost a penny yet can save you thousands of dollars' worth of mistakes, time, and headaches.
Fundamentals for Factors
Risk Management Tools

Communication with Debtors

Any time a client tells a debtor not to speak to the factor, and especially tells the factor not to speak with the debtor "for any reason," the client is simply up to no good.
Factoring Case Studies, 2nd edition
Shifty Shuffles Staffing Services

As the factor who owns the receivables, unless you have agreed to a complete non-notification relationship, you have every right to contact a debtor any time you feel the need.
Factoring Case Studies, 2nd edition
Shifty Shuffles Staffing Services

Debtor avoidance of the factor often means they've paid the client and don't want to face you. When this happens to you, consider it a blaring alarm warning you to act *now* (not later) to take whatever action necessary to get your money back.
Factoring Case Studies, 2nd edition
Hardluck Harvey's Homes

This case study is yet another lesson (when short payments happen, especially consistently) in asking the *debtor* why they haven't paid the invoice in full or at all. Don't ask the client and expect a truthful answer when you are already suspicious of him. Further, don't just use escrow reserves to recoup your advances and discounts, and consider the matter settled. If there is a consistent reason why invoices aren't paid in full, the sooner you know the real reason why – from the debtor – the better.

Factoring Case Studies, 2nd edition
Damon Deevyus, LLC

Concentrations

Without question, avoiding over concentrations is by far the most important safeguard you can implement. If you religiously follow all other risk management practices but overlook this one, you can still lose big time and be out of business in a heartbeat.

How to Run a Small Factoring Business
Reducing Your Risk

Over concentration – the mistake of having too much money in one client, customer, and/or invoice – is far and away the biggest reason factors lose money and even go out of business, regardless of their size.

Fundamentals for Factors
Risk Management Tools

Whatever you do, no matter what size your operation is, avoid over concentrations. Don't invest more than you can afford to lose in any client, customer, or invoice. That simple procedure does not cost a penny, yet it can save you thousands upon thousands of dollars – and even save your company.

How to Run a Small Factoring Business
Additional Resources: A Small Factor's Thoughts about Big Factors' Concerns

The greatest risk factors of *any* size face is not fraud: it is over concentration. Factors with too much of their capital invested in any one client, customer, or even invoice run the risk of serious or even catastrophic loss.

How to Run a Small Factoring Business
Additional Resources: A Small Factor's Thoughts about Big Factors' Concerns

A heavy concentration in one customer can lead to a bitter ending, even if that concentration is with a state or other government entity.

Factoring Case Studies, 2nd edition
Dunfore Day Care

In the great majority of cases when factors close their doors or merge with another factor, the primary cause can be traced to losses where the factors were over-concentrated.

Fundamentals for Factors
Risk Management Tools

Construction Receivables

While there are many subcontractors who will benefit from factoring, those who buy their paper absolutely must know how to do so properly and safely. Entering this arena without any experience in construction is opening your door to problems.

Fundamentals for Factors
Receivables to Avoid

Converting Payments

The other most common fraudulent activity factoring clients may commit is to convert customer checks which pay factored invoices. In other words, instead of a check going to the factor, the business owner obtains a customer's check for a factored invoice and deposits or cashes it.

Factoring: Sell Your Invoices Today, Get Cash Tomorrow
Faulty Assumptions and Mistakes to Avoid

Clearly state in your contract a 15% penalty is charged (on the invoice amount or check amount, whichever is larger) if a client deposits or cashes a factored payment. If he converts a check, pays the penalty,

and wants to continue factoring, chances are very good it won't happen again.
How to Run a Small Factoring Business
Common Mistakes

What always amazes me about clients who divert checks is they inexplicably assume I won't find out. Do they really think I won't notice a payment is long overdue? Tracking receivables I've bought is what I do for a living! What do they think I do all day, watch soap operas and eat cookies?
How to Run a Small Factoring Business
Common Mistakes

Cost of Factoring

Let's get right to the point here: is factoring more expensive than bank loans? Yes. Is factoring "too expensive"? Well…compared to what? Bank loans you can't get?
Top 10 Misconceptions about Factoring
#3: "Factoring Is Too Expensive"

If factoring costs less than the income it generates, *and* improves a company's bottom line, *and* increases its production, *and* enables growth…so what if it's "more expensive" than a bank loan?
Factoring: Sell Your Invoices Today, Get Cash Tomorrow
Why Haven't I Heard of This Before?

If sales jump with increased cash flow, factoring can more than pay for itself.
Factoring: Sell Your Invoices Today, Get Cash Tomorrow
Faulty Assumptions and Mistakes to Avoid

The correct question is not, "What is the interest you're charging?" because that's simply a red herring. The correct question is, "Can I take the cash generated from factoring and use it to earn more than I'm paying for it?"
Factoring: Sell Your Invoices Today, Get Cash Tomorrow
Faulty Assumptions and Mistakes to Avoid

The significant question for companies considering factoring is not, "How much does factoring cost?" but "Will factoring generate more income than it costs?" If the answer is yes, the decision to factor is one of simple arithmetic.

Factoring: Sell Your Invoices Today, Get Cash Tomorrow
Faulty Assumptions and Mistakes to Avoid

If using these services (billing, A/R collections follow-up, credit screening, and so on) enable you to eliminate these tasks from in-house staff, you'll lower your expenses and/or give your staff other responsibilities. This can improve your profit margin in addition to increasing sales. Therefore you need to consider not only the costs of factoring, but the benefits as well.

Factoring: Sell Your Invoices Today, Get Cash Tomorrow
Faulty Assumptions and Mistakes to Avoid

Crooks

Are there crooks out there who want your money and are remarkably clever at getting their hands on it? Absolutely. Are there people who are dishonest to the core and don't have the slightest hesitation or sense of guilt about deceiving you in order to clean out your bank account? You better believe it. Are there people who are just plain bad and delight in outsmarting you and grabbing your money and disappearing? Yes, no question about it.

Top 10 Illusions about Risk and Loss
#9: Most Losses Result from Intentional Fraud by People Who Are Crooks

Most losses I have experienced in my factoring business don't result from intentional fraud by crooks. Those cases happen, make no mistake about it; but they are actually pretty few and far between.

Top 10 Illusions about Risk and Loss
#9: Most Losses Result from Intentional Fraud by People Who Are Crooks

While I haven't kept statistical records, I would guess that for every one case of an outright crook who plans with malice aforethought to steal your money, there are 10, 20 or maybe even 50 good clients whose accounts go bad for any of a multitude of reasons, and the result is the loss of your money. Most factoring losses come about this way – not from "bad guys."

Top 10 Illusions about Risk and Loss
#9: Most Losses Result from Intentional Fraud by People Who Are Crooks

Avoiding larger invoice and client volume decreases your exposure to sophisticated criminals who are drawn to large amounts of money like bugs to a spotlight.

Fundamentals for Factors
Risk Management Tools

Customer Payments

Be clear from the beginning that payments will always come to you or you won't be able to be their factor. Sweet and simple.

How to Run a Small Factoring Business
Common Mistakes

If payments end up in the hands of the client for any reason, you must be in direct contact with the person in authority at the customer's company. Make it clear payments must be sent to you alone, and only you can release the NOA. If payments continue to go to the client, stop buying invoices to this customer. If this is a problem with other customers of a client, stop funding the client altogether.

Top 10 Illusions about Risk and Loss
#7: Once a Customer Receives a Notice of Assignment, Sending Payment to the Factor as Instructed Will Not Be a Problem

Customer Reactions to Factoring

A common concern among many business owners who consider factoring their receivables is their customers' reaction. They might worry, "Will they think I'm in financial trouble?" "Will they stop doing business with me?" "Will they refuse to pay a factor?" While these concerns are not uncommon, the vast majority of the time they are quite groundless, as is soon discovered.

Factoring: Sell Your Invoices Today, Get Cash Tomorrow
Telling Your Customers

When a company factors its receivables, "what their customers think" about their financial stability is simply and completely irrelevant. The truth is, they just don't think about it at all.

Top 10 Misconceptions about Factoring
#1: "When a Company Factors, Customers Will Think It's in Financial Trouble"

Good business owners appreciate the need for cash to run a company, and chances are good if a customer resists working with your factor, you have experienced other issues with this customer that make him less than ideal.

Factoring: Sell Your Invoices Today, Get Cash Tomorrow
Telling Your Customers

Customers to Factor (Bad)

If your customer is financially shaky or has been slippery about payments in the past, your invoices to him are not good candidates for factoring.

Factoring: Sell Your Invoices Today, Get Cash Tomorrow
Faulty Assumptions and Mistakes to Avoid

Factoring poor-paying customers makes your cash flow even worse in the long run.

Factoring: Sell Your Invoices Today, Get Cash Tomorrow
Faulty Assumptions and Mistakes to Avoid

You must impress on new clients which customers they should factor, and which they should not. If customers pay late, or partially, or erratically, both the client and factor end up regretting factoring them.
Factoring Case Studies, 2nd edition
Dorrie Nobb Advertising

Factoring Case Studies, 2nd edition
Dorrie Nobb Advertising

Because business owners receive immediate cash when they sell their invoices, at first some think, "Boy, it would sure be nice to get cash for these bad accounts and not have to mess with them anymore." Unfortunately, such thinking couldn't be more wrong: those slowest paying and deadbeat customers are the absolute *worst* accounts a company can factor.
Top 10 Misconceptions about Factoring
#8: "You Should Factor Your Slowest Paying and Deadbeat Customers";
Alternate: "Factors Are Like Collection Agencies"

Customers to Factor (Good)

Factoring works best when the invoices you sell are to dependable, stable, creditworthy customers. These are the customers who don't pay you immediately, but will definitely pay you.
Factoring: Sell Your Invoices Today, Get Cash Tomorrow
Faulty Assumptions and Mistakes to Avoid

Whether your factor operates on a recourse or non-recourse basis, only sell invoices which you are confident will pay in a timely manner.
Factoring: Sell Your Invoices Today, Get Cash Tomorrow
What to Look for in a Factor

You must impress on new clients which customers they should factor, and which they should not. They should factor only those whom they are confident will pay in a timely fashion, and in full.
Factoring Case Studies, 2nd edition
Dorrie Nobb Advertising

Review your customer list and look for those who cause you the least grief, take around a month or so to pay, and pay dependably. Factoring these will help grow your business steadily and dependably.
Top 10 Misconceptions about Factoring
#8: "You Should Factor Your Slowest Paying and Deadbeat Customers";
Alternate: "Factors Are Like Collection Agencies"

It is far better for both the factor and the business owner to buy and sell receivables that are steady, dependable, and typically pay within two to six weeks without any follow up. Those that pay around 30 days are optimal.

Top 10 Misconceptions about Factoring
#8: "You Should Factor Your Slowest Paying and Deadbeat Customers"; Alternate: "Factors Are Like Collection Agencies"

Customer Payment Websites

Ask about payment websites, especially with government and very large customers. More and more organizations have these sites. Using them is a tremendous risk mitigator for any factor. Always ask very early (of both the prospect and the customer) if the debtor has a web site to track payments and/or other AP functions.

Factoring Case Studies, 2nd edition
Slimegall Medical Transport

Do the Right Thing

Factors cannot assume a particular client will do the right thing because it is the right thing. The need for money trumps what is right just about every time.

Factoring Case Studies, 2nd edition
Dee Seetful and Associates

I have learned that a client's type of business, position in the community, or personal faith has no bearing on whether they will be honest. In the long run, these mean nothing when it comes to predicting who will do the right thing.

Factoring Case Studies, 2nd edition
Dee Seetful and Associates

Due Diligence

The purpose of due diligence is to *reduce* risk. Nothing can completely *eliminate* it.

How to Run a Small Factoring Business
Due Diligence

When deciding how much due diligence to perform in your business, perhaps the best question is this: "What is adequate due diligence for *my* peace of mind with *this* particular client?"
How to Run a Small Factoring Business
Due Diligence

There are four general steps of due diligence. They include:
    A. Determining if a client is one you wish to factor.
    B. Determining if a customer is one you wish to factor.
    C. Determining if a new invoice is one you wish to factor.
    D. Taking action to secure payment on overdue invoices.
Fundamentals for Factors
Risk Management Tools

When doing your underwriting, you are attempting to put a jigsaw puzzle together. Each part of your due diligence creates a piece of that puzzle, which you then piece together to form an overall picture of the desirability of a prospective client.
Top 10 Insights about Factoring Prospects
What Does My Due Diligence Tell Me about This Individual's Personal Character?

As you read the report ask yourself, "What is the general picture painted in this credit report? How stable is this business? Is this someone who will pay his bills? How long will he probably take to pay? Do I want to wait that long?"
How to Run a Small Factoring Business
Common Mistakes

If the prospect wants you to hurry up your procedures, beware. Don't be rushed. Take the time necessary to do the due diligence you feel is needed. If the prospect isn't willing or able to wait for this, she probably won't be the kind of client with whom you want to work.
How to Run a Small Factoring Business
Common Mistakes

Be careful which clients and customers you take on, and don't get lazy with your due diligence. One hit not only can wipe out principal and profits, but it can take many months from which to recover.
How to Run a Small Factoring Business
Money

When I started factoring I was too cheap to get any credit checking or background reporting services at that time, so I was going on my gut feeling for underwriting. I would suggest using this method only if you love to lose money. The problem: the scammers are the exceptionally flattering and friendly ones.
Marketing Methods for Small Factors & Brokers
RaeLynn Schkade

Ending a Problem Factoring Relationship

When you see the writing on the wall with a problem client or debtor – especially a government with serious financial problems – don't hesitate to terminate the relationship sooner rather than later. It's not an easy decision, but it can certainly be the wise one.
Factoring Case Studies, 2nd edition
Dunfore Day Care

Expenses

Remember, one of the keys to success is keeping your overhead as low as possible. Your high returns will diminish quickly if you spend money on things you really don't need.
Fundamentals for Factors
Practical Matters: Office, Time, and Capital

Keep overhead low and don't pay for what you don't yet need, and don't go overboard on toys and gadgets. Put off expensive purchases until you really need them. Set a budget and stay within it, and modify it as time goes by and your financial picture evolves.
How I Run My One-Person Factoring Business
Key Points

You should carefully think through what you really need and keep overhead to a minimum. My rule of thumb: don't buy something until you experience the need for it at least three times; never buy ahead of time what you only *think* you will need.

How to Run a Small Factoring Business
What I've Learned about the Factoring Industry

Pay back loans/lines of credit you're not using as soon as you know you don't or won't need the cash. Don't pay for money you're not using to make money.

How to Run a Small Factoring Business
Money

Factoring as a Drug

Cash is often described as the "life blood" of a business. So when a company waits a long time for customers to pay, a business could be described as "cash anemic" and in need of cash infusions. In this case, factoring can be the medication needed to make the company well again; it can be "just what the doctor ordered."

Top 10 Misconceptions about Factoring
#4: "Once You Start Factoring You Can't Stop"; Alternate: "Factoring Is Like a Drug and Your Company Will Get Addicted"

Many companies factor because they have "anemic" cash flow, receivables that take longer to pay than their operating costs can tolerate, or they're losing business by not offering terms to larger customers. Their business is "sick" and needs "medicine" that will make it better. When used properly by the business owner and not abused, the prescription of factoring can be extremely effective.

Top 10 Misconceptions about Factoring
#4: "Once You Start Factoring You Can't Stop"; Alternate: "Factoring Is Like a Drug and Your Company Will Get Addicted"

Factoring, just like medication, is abused when it's not used according to directions. Business owners who use factoring funds to buy personal toys that don't help the business are misusing the medicine. The medication – cash – is not being used for its intended purpose, healing the company.

Top 10 Misconceptions about Factoring
#4: "Once You Start Factoring You Can't Stop"; Alternate: "Factoring Is Like a Drug and Your Company Will Get Addicted"

Likewise, business owners who give the factor phony invoices, invoices for work not completed, submit double billings for the same job, misdirect and deposit factored payments, or commit other acts of fraud, are not only misusing factoring – they're committing a criminal offense. Just like someone trying to get multiple refills on a single prescription that doesn't allow it, they're not using the medication properly and are going to get themselves in trouble.

Top 10 Misconceptions about Factoring
#4: "Once You Start Factoring You Can't Stop"; Alternate: "Factoring Is Like a Drug and Your Company Will Get Addicted"

In my experience, business owners who abuse factoring, much like a drug addict, usually wind up in a downward spiral that too often ends the life of the business.

Top 10 Misconceptions about Factoring
#4: "Once You Start Factoring You Can't Stop"; Alternate: "Factoring Is Like a Drug and Your Company Will Get Addicted"

Factoring can be like a prescription drug, but prescription drugs are not bad in and of themselves. When used correctly they can provide remarkable curative powers, and provide for the long-term health of the person (or business) using them. Misused or abused, both can have negative results – however that is not the fault of the prescription. Taken properly, factoring can be like a miracle drug to many companies. When misused and abused, it can lead to their downfall.

Top 10 Misconceptions about Factoring
#4: "Once You Start Factoring You Can't Stop"; Alternate: "Factoring Is Like a Drug and Your Company Will Get Addicted"

Factoring Contracts

When you receive the document, an instant glance will tell you something very significant: can the font used throughout the contract be read easily? Is the font a common one (such as Ariel or Times New Roman) that is not ornate or cursive, and is its size large enough to be legible and read without difficulty? The reason for mentioning this is obvious: why would anyone provide a contract that is not easy to read?

Top 10 Questions to Ask When Looking for a Factor
#9: "Does the Factor Have Minimum Monthly Charges, a Term Contract, or Hidden Fees?"

Occasionally I've seen factoring contracts printed in a really small font that included terms, charges, and/or practices the factor probably didn't want the client to notice or understand. Contracts you can't easily read provide a warning that this may be a factor to avoid. While all contracts are written in legal jargon that sometimes only attorneys can clearly understand, at least the font should be large enough to read without a magnifying glass.

Top 10 Questions to Ask When Looking for a Factor
#9: "Does the Factor Have Minimum Monthly Charges, a Term Contract, or Hidden Fees?"

If the description of discount or fee calculation leaves your head spinning, or you simply don't understand it, think twice about signing that contract. You need to be very clear what you will be paying, and how that is calculated. It need not be complicated, but some factors seem to make it that way.

Top 10 Questions to Ask When Looking for a Factor
#9: "Does the Factor Have Minimum Monthly Charges, a Term Contract, or Hidden Fees?"

Factoring Income

You can realistically make 2½ times as much factoring $5,000 as you would referring $20,000.

How to Run a Small Factoring Business
What I've Learned about the Factoring Industry

You can make a lot of money factoring, but a single big mistake can take it all away in one fell swoop.

How to Run a Small Factoring Business
Bits of Wisdom for the Small Factor

If your only purpose is the money you make, your clients will sense this quickly or eventually learn it, and their trust in you will become shrouded.

How to Run a Small Factoring Business
What I've Learned about the Factoring Industry

Factoring Rates

Make a point of keeping all your factoring rates simple and easy to grasp. The more complex your rates, advances, and reserves, the less your client will understand what you're doing and what they're paying. This can lead not only to the client running his business blindly, but very soon, distrusting and blaming you, the factor, for everything. That's the last thing you want.

Factoring Case Studies, 2nd edition
Razzle & Dazzle Manufacturing

I am sometimes irritated by a small number of factoring companies who brashly advertise exceptionally low "teaser" rates to lure business. You don't have to search too hard on the internet to find factors who tout factoring rates of less than 1% for the first 30 days, or who give 100% advances, or who simply have rates that (after doing some homework and seeing what most rates are) appear too good to be true. Believe me, they are – especially if your business is pretty small.

Top 10 Questions to Ask When Looking for a Factor
#2: "Adding It Up: What Does This Really Cost?"

Factors simply cannot provide 100% advances and make income. This is mathematically impossible. So when you read or hear about a factor advertising 100% advances (which is not uncommon in some niches like trucking receivables), in fact what the factor is doing is deducting his discount at the front end, from the "100%" advance, rather than deducting it from the back end – the holdback reserve when an invoice is paid.

Top 10 Questions to Ask When Looking for a Factor
#2: "Adding It Up: What Does This Really Cost?"

We know that success is not about having the lowest factoring rates. Someone who is solely shopping for the cheapest rates is not our target client. We don't have the cheapest rates. We are looking for people who need fair, prompt, convenient service so they can clear their minds of their cash flow problems and get to work on running their business.

Marketing Methods for Small Factors
RaeLynn Schkade

Factoring Reports

Changing software is a major move for any factor, so if you don't like or understand the reports his software provides, chances are slim he's going to change programs. If the reports are just too confusing or cumbersome, even after the factor explains them, you may be in a constant fog regarding the status of your invoices, advances, rebates, reserves, and your account in general. Not a wonderful thought.

Top 10 Questions to Ask When Looking for a Factor
#5: "What Reports Are Provided and How Do I Get Them?"

In addition to asking how (and how often) you can obtain reports, just as significant is what the reports tell you. Ask to see some sample reports; can you understand them easily and do they make sense? If you can get plenty of reports but they all leave you completely befuddled, they're really of no value no matter how easily or frequently you can access them.

Top 10 Questions to Ask When Looking for a Factor
#5: "What Reports Are Provided and How Do I Get Them?"

Be sure you understand what reports tell you. If you don't, you will quickly be quite lost as to how much money you have outstanding, how much the factor owes you, and how much you owe the factor. The purpose of the reports is to make your financial picture quite clear. If it's still murky from these reports, you're going to wonder just what your finances are really like, and have an uneasy feeling that only the factor really knows.

Top 10 Questions to Ask When Looking for a Factor
#5: "What Reports Are Provided and How Do I Get Them?"

Factoring Volume

Larger factors willing to accept clients factoring $10,000 want them to grow, and grow quickly. They need them to reach the point where the income their account generates is profitable. If a very small client doesn't grow in the time frame expected, the larger factor will frequently let the client go because the volume just isn't worth the factor's time and expense.

Top 10 Questions to Ask When Looking for a Factor
#10: "Is the Factor Suited to the Size of My Company?"

My rule of thumb is always this: "Don't pay for money you don't need."

Top 10 Questions to Ask When Looking for a Factor
#8: Do I Have to Factor Everything?

Factors, Features

There are many features in a factor to consider. These features include the niche or niches a factor serves, factoring dollar volume required, services provided, and more.

Factoring: Sell Your Invoices Today, Get Cash Tomorrow
What to Look for in a Factor

Factors, Larger

If you intend to enter those deeper waters, you need financial capability, adequate legal representation – and you need the stomach for the risks involved with transactions involving a lot of zeros.

How to Run a Small Factoring Business
Additional Resources: A Small Factor's Thoughts about Big Factors' Concerns

Factors, Longevity

A factoring company's longevity means absolutely nothing when it comes to providing good service, fair rates and practices, and ability to simply do the job. Every company needs to stay on the cutting edge of their industry to remain sharp and competitive.

Factoring Case Studies, 2nd edition
Dameon Deevyus, LLC

Factors, New

Working as an independent small factor will cost virtually nothing to get started, other than the operating capital you need to buy invoices. Your available funds can be put to work immediately and will quickly generate income.

Fundamentals for Factors
Is Factoring Right for You?

Especially during your learning and beginning period, you may take a hit or two because of the "Newbie" tattoo etched on your forehead for all to see, especially clients. A few of them will not be honest and try to capitalize on your greenhorn status.

How I Run My One-Person Factoring Business
Key Points

Don't beat yourself up when you make a mistake, bad decision, or get burned. Expect to take occasional losses and structure your business with this expectation. Learn from unfortunate experiences and don't repeat the actions that led to them. Bad experiences are your teachers, not marks of failure.

How I Run My One-Person Factoring Business
Key Points

Numerous risks go with factoring – dishonest, selfish, careless, and otherwise untrustworthy clients and customers, and errors in procedures or judgment made by many factors. Therefore common sense suggests a factor's foremost strategy is to set financial limits, thereby putting minimal amounts at risk. This is especially prudent when the factor is new, even if his or her pool of factoring funds is sizeable.
Factoring Case Studies (2nd Edition)
Assessment

Rome wasn't built in a day; likewise, your factoring business won't take root and flourish instantly. Expect to take at least 6 to 24 months for your business to become established, create a modest book of business, and finally take hold.
How I Run My One-Person Factoring Business
Key Points

Learning the ropes is best done with small accounts and small volumes. Feed yourself in small spoonfuls while you're learning to eat.
How to Run a Small Factoring Business
Bits of Wisdom for the Small Factor

Don't try to grow too fast. Just like a baby, allow yourself a good year to learn how to walk in this business.
How to Run a Small Factoring Business
Money

Factors, Other

There are factors among us who have fees which are calculated – and hidden – in a myriad of devious ways, and by which an unsuspecting prospect or broker can be blind-sided when they are charged.
Top 10 Statements You Never Want to Hear
#6: "The Other Factor Had Fees They Didn't Tell Me about, and I Now Want to Come Back to You"

If another factor offers rates significantly less than yours and a client is tempted to accept, make sure the client reads – and understands – the fine print, and asks about every single little charge that is included in the other factor's offer. If your rates are competitive and the other factor has extra charges not mentioned up front, your rates may very well be every bit as good if not better.

Top 10 Statements You Never Want to Hear
#6: "The Other Factor Had Fees They Didn't Tell Me about, and I Now Want to Come Back to You"

Factors, Response Time

Nothing can be more aggravating than trying to reach the person who will be sending your advance, being unable to reach her, and waiting (what seems like an eternity) to hear back. If you have payroll coming up and you absolutely must talk to your Account Executive about some invoices you want to factor, the availability and responsiveness of that person can become critical.

Top 10 Questions to Ask When Looking for a Factor
#4: "How Long Does the Factor Take to Give Advances and Respond to My Calls?"

Factors, Small

Because you deal with both people and money, just about any kind of background will serve you well as a small factor.

Fundamentals for Factors
Is Factoring Right for You?

As a small factor, I have experienced the same trials and successes that my larger factoring colleagues experience, though mine are on a smaller scale – I have smaller clients, smaller invoices, smaller client credit lines, smaller everything. I have enjoyed very pleasant, profitable accounts, but have also been defrauded and struggled to get paid back by other clients (which often never happened). Factoring is factoring, after all. Certain things are constant no matter what the size of your operation.

How I Run My One-Person Factoring Business
Training

I have been a factor for many years. Unlike numerous factors in business this long, I have chosen to remain a very small operation. Why? Because rather than making the most money possible and

living with the responsibilities involved, remaining small is a life style choice for me. Form follows function.
How I Run My Virtual Factoring Office
My Virtual Office

Financial Advisors

Those trained to be business or financial experts often have little or no exposure to the practice of factoring, and don't completely understand it themselves.
Factoring: Sell Your Invoices Today, Get Cash Tomorrow
Why Haven't I Heard of This Before?

Financial and other professionals who intentionally do not inform business owners of factoring's availability, due to their own ignorance or outdated assumptions, do a disservice to their clients.
Factoring: Sell Your Invoices Today, Get Cash Tomorrow
Why Haven't I Heard of This Before?

If factoring will increase your bottom line, deciding not to factor will actually cost your company money. In the sample manufacturing company's comparison cited earlier, not factoring would have cost the business $17,000 in missed opportunities. Why would someone do this? Probably because his accountant told him factoring was "too expensive."
Factoring: Sell Your Invoices Today, Get Cash Tomorrow
Faulty Assumptions and Mistakes to Avoid

Yes, factoring is more expensive than a bank loan; but "too expensive"? If it can help or even save the business, the financial professional needs to carefully distinguish between sound advice and personal bias.
Top 10 Misconceptions about Factoring
#3: "Factoring Is Too Expensive"

Focus

I have learned that as I stay focused on other people's needs, I make much more money than when I am focused on making money.
Marketing Methods for Small Factors & Brokers
RaeLynn Schkade

Following Your Rules

Your greatest weapon for avoiding a catastrophic loss is a simple, cost-free procedure: set credit limits with clients and customers, and limit the size of invoices you buy. Then *stay within these limits and do not make exceptions.*
Factoring Case Studies (2nd Edition)
Assessment

Establish and test your parameters, limits, types of businesses you'll fund, and whom you'll turn away and why. Once you have a good set of guidelines, **follow them.**
How to Run a Small Factoring Business
Common Mistakes

First and foremost, create policies and procedures with which you are comfortable and then do not deviate from them. If you do (and come on, we all do), be sure you effectively communicate this is an *exception* to an established rule.
Factoring Case Studies, 2nd edition
Clank Brothers Wiring and Cable

When you act wisely and develop – and follow – sound investment safeguards, you cannot have a catastrophic loss. It's only when you don't develop, maintain, and follow these safeguards that your factoring investment comes into serious jeopardy.
Fundamentals for Factors
Risk Management Tools

Follow Up Calls

If a customer is on a 30 day term but never pays until about day 50, be sure the factor knows this so she doesn't start calling on day 31. If someone routinely pays in a couple weeks, be sure the factor knows this too so she can act appropriately when invoices are 35 days old – late for this customer. In short, consider your factor a teammate when it comes to collecting payments. You both want invoices to be paid in a timely manner, and you don't want to unnecessarily irritate a good customer by phone calls arriving prior to their normal payment times.
Top 10 Questions to Ask When Looking for a Factor
#6: "What Happens When My Customer Doesn't Pay?"

Take action when you notice something has changed slightly: payments are not as regular, or in the amounts you expect, or start taking longer and longer to pay than they once did. When any of these happen, call the debtor immediately and find out why.

Factoring Case Studies, 2nd edition
Hardluck Harvey's Homes

I learned some time ago not to rely on most clients to do follow up calls. They are too busy, it's not a job they enjoy, and/or their personality is such that being hard-nosed with customers is not in their nature. They are afraid of alienating a customer and losing the business. Most clients are usually more than happy to let you be their collections department, as long as you're professional about it and don't bully their customers.

How to Run a Small Factoring Business
Additional Resources: The Secret to Getting Paid

Professional follow up calls are one of the most important services you can offer as a small factor. It's also one of the most important tasks you must constantly stay on top of. Do you need to be nasty? No. Do you need to be persistent and consistent? No question.

How to Run a Small Factoring Business
Additional Resources: The Secret to Getting Paid

I say to clients with slow payers, "I have another client who is always paid in 45 days or less, and usually less." The others are in awe and want to know his secret. "Call every customer who hasn't paid you at 35 days, and get the date when your check is going to be cut. If they don't pay according to terms, stop working for them or put them on COD." Unfortunately many are reluctant to do this. They say they're afraid of losing business or that a huge corporate customer will ignore them or won't keep them as a vendor, which may occasionally be true. But I think more often they just don't want to take the time, or don't want to seem like a hard nose. They're too nice.

How to Run a Small Factoring Business
Additional Resources: The Secret to Getting Paid

Fraud

Fraud on the part of your client is an unhappy but real possibility you must acknowledge and guard against. Examples include:

A. The client receives payments for factored invoices and does not forward these payments to you.

B. The client factors invoices for which work has not been completed or product has not been delivered.

C. The invoice a client sends a customer has the client's address for remittance, but the invoice he provides the factor has the factor's address for remittance.

D. The client instructs a customer that he is no longer factoring, and/or instructs a customer that payments for factored invoices should be re-routed to him.

E. Collusion on the part of the client and customer.

F. Collusion on the part of the client who creates and factors outright phony invoices with a bogus customer.

G. The client claims to own a company, but in fact there is no company and no customer.

Fundamentals for Factors
Factoring Risks

Clients who intentionally factor fraudulent invoices are committing criminal behavior and are subject to serious penalties.

Factoring: Sell Your Invoices Today, Get Cash Tomorrow
Faulty Assumptions and Mistakes to Avoid

Factors can only buy good invoices for work completed – not invoices "being generated from proposals for work not yet started, let alone completed." Submitting such "invoices" (which is fraud) and funding them (which should never be done) is the kiss of death for a factoring relationship.

Factoring Case Studies, 2nd edition
Clank Brothers Wiring and Cable

The other most common fraudulent activity factoring clients may commit is to convert customer checks which pay factored invoices. In other words, instead of a check going to the factor, the business owner obtains a customer's check for a factored invoice and deposits or cashes it.

Factoring: Sell Your Invoices Today, Get Cash Tomorrow
Faulty Assumptions and Mistakes to Avoid

Any time a client tells a debtor not to speak to the factor, and especially tells the factor not to speak with the debtor "for any reason," the client is simply up to no good.

Factoring Case Studies, 2nd edition
Shifty Shuffles Staffing Services

Why would a client tell you, "Don't contact this customer about his late payments"? The answer is simple. Either...

    a) he's factored a phony invoice and doesn't want you to find out; or

    b) he's already received payment for the invoice and copped the check, and doesn't want you to find out.

Top 10 Statements You Never Want to Hear
#3: "Don't Contact This Customer about His Late Payments"

This statement is one you never want to hear if it is a customer's reply to your inquiry about unpaid invoices you factored but didn't verify before advancing funds.

Top 10 Statements You Never Want to Hear
#7: "We've Never Heard of Nor Dealt with Any Company by That Name"

I never cease to be amazed at how blasé so many clients can be when they receive a check for factored invoices, and deposit the check without much of a thought. Even more, even when they have been told this action is completely unacceptable, many still consider converting checks as no big deal – even after being clearly told they just committed fraud.

Factoring Case Studies, 2nd edition
Blahzay Auto Transport

Assuming someone will be honest because he has a family is just as erroneous as assuming someone will not defraud you because she teaches classes in business ethics. You might as well think someone won't defraud you because the person has brown eyes.
Factoring Case Studies, 2nd edition
Shifty Shuffles Staffing Services

Be clear: *anyone* can cheat you. Anyone.
Factoring Case Studies, 2nd edition
Shifty Shuffles Staffing Services

Every now and then you have an account in which a seemingly remarkable series of misfortunes strikes an unlucky client. While such things certainly can happen, when they get to the point they are "unbelievable," they probably are. People who divert checks and otherwise steal funds you are due can be remarkably creative in the stories they come up with.
Factoring Case Studies, 2nd edition
Hardluck Harvey's Homes

The act of fraud can be very blurry in the eyes of a client.
Factoring Case Studies, 2nd edition
Budibuddy Metal Fabrication

Go Wrong

The question is not so much a matter of *if* something will go wrong from time to time with your clients – but *what*.
Top 10 Insights about Factoring Prospects
#3: What Can Go Wrong With This Deal?

Sometimes people new to factoring are a bit startled at the thought of something going wrong with an account. They rather innocently ask the simple question, "What can go wrong?" Quite honestly, I'm never sure how to answer that question. It's like being asked, "What can go wrong with a marriage?"
Top 10 Insights about Factoring Prospects
#3: What Can Go Wrong With This Deal?

Could things have gone south with this deal? Things can go south with *any* deal.
Factoring Case Studies, 2nd edition
Safensound Janitorial and Maintenance

Greed

Don't get greedy – ever!
How to Run a Small Factoring Business
Bits of Wisdom for the Small Factor

For those who wish to factor successfully, they must find a middle ground where sound business practices, prudence and common sense overcome greed or excessive generosity.
Fundamentals for Factors
Factoring Risks

Helping Clients

Who's first on your list of priorities? If it's not the client, you will have far fewer.
How to Run a Small Factoring Business
Bits of Wisdom for the Small Factor

As long as you make enough to help clients, run your own business, and get ahead, that's what it's all about. Plus your clients will look upon you as a people person interested in helping them, rather than a number cruncher who makes decisions hunched over a calculator. In their position, which kind of person would you rather deal with?
How to Run a Small Factoring Business
Money

The overriding reason to be in the factoring business is to help your clients.
How to Run a Small Factoring Business
Bits of Wisdom for the Small Factor

You not only benefit the small business owner by relieving him or her of a great deal of stress caused by inadequate cash flow, but you often provide the cash for payroll which puts food on the tables of clients' employees. You are providing help to more people than you may even be aware.
Fundamentals for Factors
Is Factoring Right for You?

Hidden Fees

Read the contract very carefully, and if it is printed with an especially small font which makes reading it difficult, read it all the more carefully. This is especially true when it comes to miscellaneous fees and charges. These are known as "hidden fees" which somehow just aren't mentioned until you get the contract (or later). However, even then, some factors might say they have "no hidden fees" but when you get the contract, you may find hidden fees simply called something else – like a "good faith deposit" for example.
Top 10 Questions to Ask When Looking for a Factor
#9: "Does the Factor Have Minimum Monthly Charges, a Term Contract, or Hidden Fees?"

When a factor has exceptionally low discounts, look very carefully for hidden fees: some are called by various names, some simply aren't mentioned. Most factors will charge for out of pocket expenses like wire fees (which normally shouldn't be more than about $25, and preferably less). Look for any fee not mentioned on their website, by their sales person, or that just doesn't come up until you're unexpectedly dinged.
Top 10 Questions to Ask When Looking for a Factor
#9: "Does the Factor Have Minimum Monthly Charges, a Term Contract, or Hidden Fees?"

Charging many extra fees is simply a means for factors with very low advertised discount rates to increase their income. Thus the total cost of using them is more in line with what other factors charge (and all must charge) to be profitable.
Top 10 Questions to Ask When Looking for a Factor
#9: "Does the Factor Have Minimum Monthly Charges, a Term Contract, or Hidden Fees?"

Factors who claim ultra-low rates invariably also have various and often numerous hidden fees and charges to make up for what their discounts don't earn to pay their bills.

Top 10 Questions to Ask When Looking for a Factor
#2: "Adding It Up: What Does This Really Cost?"

Human Nature

If you don't understand what people are really like deep down, the heavy dose of human nature you'll receive from factoring will be quite an eye-opener.

Factoring Case Studies (2nd Edition)
Introduction

I have found when you deal with people's money, you are handling something that over time reveals their inner nature.

Factoring Case Studies (2nd Edition)
Introduction

Improving Cash Flow

Accepting credit cards for consumer and some government and business accounts, in tandem with factoring for other government and business accounts, make a great combination and can greatly improve your cash flow.

Factoring: Sell Your Invoices Today, Get Cash Tomorrow
Faulty Assumptions and Mistakes to Avoid

Instincts

If you ever get an uneasy feeling about someone, follow your instincts and avoid him like the plague.

Fundamentals for Factors
Risk Management Tools

Listen to your instincts when you sense a client is going to do something devious, and pay very close attention to anything every Accounts Payable person says about any client.

Factoring Case Studies, 2nd edition
Damon Deevyus, LLC

Never hush that little voice. If your little voice is throwing a temper tantrum, listen to it. Even if you aren't exactly sure what it is trying to tell you, listen to the fact that it is present. Do not let a client's or broker's urgency make you second guess yourself when funding. If your hand starts to shake as it hovers over the send button, don't press the send button.
Factoring Case Studies, 2nd edition
Clank Brothers Wiring and Cable

Invoices, Batching

Batching invoices when you can track every invoice that has been batched, or at least know when part of a batch of invoices is not going to be paid, can work. But when you have no idea which invoices and/or batches you're being paid for – and which ones aren't being paid at all – the result is that invoices appear to be paying more and more slowly. It's only a matter of time before you realize you're in the deep, dark hole and can't get out of it.
Factoring Case Studies, 2nd edition
Slimegall Medical Transport

Legal System

Personally, I like working with little guys. They suit me just fine. I also like the idea of never paying five figures in legal fees.
How to Run a Small Factoring Business
Additional Resources: A Small Factor's Thoughts about Big Factors' Concerns

If a client digs in her heels and resolutely determines she is *not* going to pay you, even if you're in the right and the money is justly owed and all your ducks are lined up, the deck is still stacked in *her* favor, not yours. Collection laws tie the hands of your collection agency's efforts, and recouping your money through the courts will be a long, tedious, expensive, and unpleasant experience. You need to be owed a heck of a lot of money to make pursuing its recovery through the legal system worthwhile. And even then there are no guarantees you'll win, nor if you win, that you'll actually get your money back.
Top 10 Statements You Never Want to Hear
#1: "I Have No Intention of Paying You Back"

Don't expect the legal system to protect you. Too often it protects only those who have the most money to pay attorneys.
Factoring Case Studies, 2^(nd) edition
Smallfrey Alarm Company

Dealing with someone's attorney often means you're likely to incur some serious expenses trying to recoup your money.
Factoring Case Studies, 2^(nd) edition
Smallfrey Alarm Company

A person does something questionable or wrong. The person hires a lawyer to defend him, and the attorney comes up with a justification or a legal maneuver (or numerous legal maneuvers) to absolve his client of responsibility. This has nothing to do with making sure that true justice prevails, but with protecting the person or company paying the attorney to get the wrongdoer off the hook.
Factoring Case Studies, 2^(nd) edition
Mr. Scumbucket Janitorial Company

Don't expect the law to work in your favor when someone is dishonest or defrauds you. You will have many long, slow, arduous, steep hills to climb, and the chances of being made whole are quite frankly pretty slim.
Top 10 Illusions about Risk and Loss
#4: The Law Is in Your Favor When a Client Is Dishonest

The law is not in your favor when it comes to getting your money back from a client, no matter how badly you've been victimized and how innocent you are of any wrongdoing. If the law works at all for you, it will take a very long, tedious time and you certainly have no guarantee you'll end up with a smile on your face and a feeling of satisfaction when all is said and done. In fact, it's just about guaranteed that will be the last thing you'll have.
Top 10 Illusions about Risk and Loss
#4: The Law Is in Your Favor When a Client Is Dishonest

Letting Down Your Guard

Continue to maintain low exposures, never let your guard down, and never assume your procedures make you invincible. Factoring

involves risk; therefore you must follow specific strategies to minimize your risk at all times.
Factoring Case Studies, 2nd edition
Assessment

Things can go south on you rather quickly; they can even go south with a formerly good client you've had for a very long time. So never let down your guard.
Factoring Case Studies, 2nd edition
Claire's Repairs

Limits

One of the simplest means of avoiding a catastrophic loss is to limit your exposure to clients, customers, and invoices.
Fundamentals for Factors
Risk Management Tools

Numerous risks go with factoring – dishonest, selfish, careless, and otherwise untrustworthy clients and customers, and errors in procedures or judgment made by factors. Therefore common sense suggests a factor's foremost strategy is to set financial limits, thereby putting minimal amounts at risk. This is especially prudent when the factor is new, even if his or her pool of factoring funds is sizeable.
Factoring Case Studies (2nd Edition)
Assessment

If you increase a client's credit limit, do so in relatively small increments only after clients have proven to be honest and customers payments have proven to be dependable.
Factoring Case Studies (2nd Edition)
Assessment

Set an absolute ceiling which no client's credit limit will exceed. If a client outgrows this limit, broker him to a larger factor and continue to earn commissions, or participate with another factor and share the income (and risk). While using this strategy will not prevent losses, you will avoid catastrophic events fatal to your business. This is the simplest yet most often overlooked (or ignored) risk management tool that any factor can employ.

Factoring Case Studies, 2nd edition
Assessment

Your greatest weapon for avoiding a catastrophic loss is a simple, cost-free procedure: set credit limits with clients and customers, and limit the size of invoices you buy. Then *stay within these limits and do not make exceptions.*

Factoring Case Studies, 2nd edition
Assessment

Little Voice

Never hush that little voice. If your little voice is throwing a temper tantrum, *listen to it.* Even if you aren't exactly sure what it is trying to tell you, listen to the fact that it is present. Do not let a client's or broker's urgency make you second guess yourself when funding. If your hand starts to shake as it hovers over the send button, don't press the send button.

Factoring Case Studies, 2nd edition
Clank Brothers Wiring and Cable

Loans to Clients

You can make much better returns as a factor than as a lender, and you are wise to never give factoring clients loans in the first place.

Top 10 Statements You Never Want to Hear
#5: "Can You Loan Me Some Money to Get Through This Tight Spot?"

If you start loaning money, you won't make as much in interest as you would from factoring (even if they pay you back). And you'll have less factoring money available.

How to Run a Small Factoring Business
Common Mistakes

If you give a client a loan, his customers and receivables are not going to pay you back – *he* is (or isn't). And because his credit is likely to be poor, you have a much better chance of not getting repaid on such loans. After all, the banks (who are in the business of making loans) already told him no, probably more than once, and for good reason.

Top 10 Statements You Never Want to Hear
#5: "Can You Loan Me Some Money to Get Through This Tight Spot?"

If you give in to a client's request for a loan and you are fortunate enough to be repaid, you have set a precedent. That means chances are very good he will come back to the well again. Give a client a loan once, and you are inviting him to do it again and again.

Top 10 Statements You Never Want to Hear
#5: "Can You Loan Me Some Money to Get Through This Tight Spot?"

Loan Sharks

Because factors provide funds to companies that banks decline, it's only natural that factoring discounts are higher than bank loan interest. However, discount rates don't come close to interest charged by loan sharks. Anyone who equates the two simply does not understand factoring thoroughly, and casts an unfair pall upon the factoring industry. But because factors fund companies at higher rates than banks do, the moniker is unfortunately applied too easily.

Top 10 Misconceptions about Factoring
#10: "Factors Are Loan Sharks"

Are factoring discounts rates higher than bank interest rates? No question. Are they comparable to true loan shark interest rates? Nowhere close.

Top 10 Misconceptions about Factoring
#10: "Factors Are Loan Sharks"

Lockbox

A lockbox is usually a post office box that is completely managed by the bank. Every business day a bank employee or courier picks up the lockbox mail and delivers it to the bank's processing center, where it's opened, scanned, endorsed, and deposited directly into your account.
How I Run My One-Person Factoring Business
Tools

By early afternoon, all the day's receipts are deposited in my bank account (though I literally haven't touched a single check). I have spent 0 seconds getting the mail, opening it, preparing deposits, endorsing checks, driving to the bank, making the deposit, and driving home.
How I Run My One-Person Factoring Business
Tools

I consider my lockbox to not only be a wonderfully convenient time-saver and easy way to bank, but also a very inexpensive employee. Hiring someone to do these tasks would be much more expensive than the cost of the lock box.
How I Run My One-Person Factoring Business
Tools

A bank lockbox was not something I used for quite some time, but when my business volume reached a certain point and I learned the cost of a lockbox and what it could do for me, I started using one. Now it is one of the most important time- and money-saving tools I utilize. It also enables me to get away for trips out of town without the slightest worry about one of the most important parts of my business: daily bank deposits
How I Run My One-Person Factoring Business
Tools

Losses

Over time virtually all factors experience financial losses. This goes with the territory and must be accepted by everyone entering the field at any level. The key is to keep these losses small and non-catastrophic.

Fundamentals for Factors
The Past, Present, and Future of Factoring

Expect to take occasional losses and structure your business with this expectation. Learn from unfortunate experiences and don't repeat the actions that led to them. Bad experiences are your teachers, not marks of failure.

How I Run My One-Person Factoring Business
Key Points

If you intentionally limit the size of your client and customer credit limits, and the size of invoices you buy – and most important, *abide* by those limits – your chances of a catastrophic loss are diminished to nearly zero.

How to Run a Small Factoring Business
Additional Resources: A Small Factor's Thoughts about Big Factors' Concerns

When dealing with your normal, ordinary everyday clients, always stay alert to anomalies in advance requests and customer payment patterns of every single client. Don't let slow payments slide without good follow up, don't keep advancing funds when an account seems to be turning into a problem, and don't get lazy. Not minding the store (your job) is when most losses occur.

Top 10 Illusions about Risk and Loss
#9: Most Losses Result from Intentional Fraud by People Who Are Crooks

Loyalty

If you are putting your client's needs above your own selfish interest (notice I did not say your need to be secure and profitable; be clear about the difference) – you will develop loyalty that will pay for itself ten times more than any advertising budget.

How to Run a Small Factoring Business
Reducing Your Risk

If you make it clear by everything you say and do that your first and major concern is the success of your client's company, you will earn devoted and loyal clients, even friends, for years.
How to Run a Small Factoring Business
Bits of Wisdom for the Small Factor

If you are motivated solely by profit, you will not be a good factor, you will neither deserve nor earn your clients' loyalty, and you will not enjoy the people with whom you work.
Factoring Case Studies (2nd Edition)
Assessment

Marketing

For most new factors, marketing – finding new clients – provides the greatest challenge, especially at first. Numerous marketing methods exist and figuring out which one/s work best is usually an (unfortunately expensive) matter of trial and error. If your background provides many potential prospects in your network of business associates, friends, relatives, and other contacts, start there.
How I Run My One Person Factoring Business
Marketing: How I Keep a Steady Stream of Clients

This is the kind of work that takes months, sometimes years, for the seeds you've sown to come to fruition.
How to Run a Small Factoring Business
Common Mistakes

The seeds of marketing you sow can take many months to germinate, and often newcomers get discouraged when their efforts don't yield quick results.
How I Run My One Person Factoring Business
Marketing: How I Keep a Steady Stream of Clients

There is no silver bullet for marketing a small factoring business. In other words, no single method works 100% of the time for everyone. Some use a particular marketing strategy very successfully, while others have found the same method unrewarding.

Marketing Methods for Small Factors & Brokers
Analysis

What is your background? What do you know, what are you good at, and what do you enjoy? What types of businesses do you already know who need to improve their cash flow, and who invoice business or government customers? Who do you know that can point you toward potential clients? Begin here, and if you have enough contacts, this could be all the marketing you ever need to do, particularly if you're factoring part-time.

Fundamentals for Factors
Identifying and Locating Prospective Clients

People are more likely to do business with people they know, like, and trust, than with a stranger.

How to Run a Small Factoring Business
Bits of Wisdom for the Small Factor

What I call "acquaintance marketing" is really more educating than marketing. It costs very little or nothing, is done mostly by other people on your behalf, and brings you leads which are usually warm if not hot.

Fundamentals for Factors
Identifying and Locating Prospective Clients

One of the worst methods of marketing is trolling the waters of businesses who are already factoring, and who are, for the most part, happy with their factoring relationship.

Top 10 Statements You Never Want to Hear
#6: "The Other Factor Had Fees They Didn't Tell Me about, and I Now Want to Come Back to You"

I believe one of the best marketing strategies is not to compete with other factoring companies for the cheapest rates, but to inform and introduce your target market to the benefits of factoring. There is no

shortage of small businesses needing working capital, but not everybody knows about this financing option.
Marketing Methods for Small Factors
RaeLynn Schkade

I have found the best way to market factoring is by sharing examples of how you have helped businesses become more successful and improve their cash flow. Share a story of a specific company, and explain how cash flow shortage was hindering their growth. Explain how your business was able to provide immediate access to cash using only their invoices. A story can be a powerful example of how factoring works and can benefit small businesses.
Marketing Methods for Small Factors & Brokers
Kim Deveney

You're more likely to be successful with methods you enjoy that are an extension of your personality and skills.
How to Run a Small Factoring Business
Marketing: How to Find Clients

When you start, begin with what you are good at and *like* to do. Don't try to use a method that you inherently dislike, or at which you are decidedly untalented, whatever that may be – cold calls, public speaking, writing, whatever. I'm sure you can name it out loud. But if particular methods come naturally for you, chances are good you can use them effectively and marketing can actually be enjoyable and produce positive results.
Marketing Methods for Small Factors
Jeff Callender

You must use marketing methods that best suit your personality, skills, and interests, and you must use them constantly. Marketing, if you will, becomes a way of life.
Marketing Methods for Small Factors & Brokers
Conclusion

Decide which marketing methods will be best suited for your personality. Pick three marketing methods and stick with them for a minimum of six months before deciding if the method is working for

you. After experimenting with your top three marketing methods for six months, re-evaluate and make changes if necessary.
Marketing Methods for Small Factors & Brokers
Kim Deveney

I have seen several small businesses get "too busy to market" and they often find themselves without clients after several months of neglecting their marketing efforts. Continuous marketing efforts are extremely important to the success of your business!
Marketing Methods for Small Factors & Brokers
Kim Deveney

No matter how wonderful your website, how spectacular your brochure, or how glossy your business card, the ultimate success of your business is your relationships and how you handle them.
Marketing Methods for Small Factors & Brokers
Anne Gordon

When you belong to a networking group, get involved in that group and become known by the other members. Just joining a group really does nothing for your marketing. I volunteer at most events. That is the easiest way to become a familiar face to the rest of the organization and is much less expensive than a booth at trade shows or sponsoring some event.
Marketing Methods for Small Factors & Brokers
Anne Gordon

Integrity, fairness, caring for clients, and providing exceptional service all attract people to your business. Solid, good business practices simply make your company desirable, and thereby are an extension of marketing.
Marketing Methods for Small Factors & Brokers
Conclusion

Misdirected Payments

One of the risks of factoring is a client's intentional misdirection of payments and conversion of checks, wherein the client takes your advances, then tells a customer to send the check to him, which he deposits.

Top 10 Insights about Factoring Prospects
#3: What Can Go Wrong With This Deal?

Money

The Cardinal Rule of Money is, "Don't risk more than you can afford to lose."

How to Run a Small Factoring Business
Money

If you expect your client base to grow, be positioned to fund that growth, and you'll be a savior in their eyes. Nothing is more embarrassing or stressful than to have clients submit invoices and expect advances in 24 hours...and you can't come up with the money. If the phone or fax rings and you hope it's not a client wanting an advance, you're under funded. Believe me, that's under fun.

How to Run a Small Factoring Business
Common Mistakes

The juggling act you continually play as a factor is keeping your money on the street every day possible so that it's working for you, while taking care to not run out of funds when a client comes to you to factor another batch of invoices.

How to Run a Small Factoring Business
Money

Monitor

One of a factor's most important tasks – for both the client and the factor – is monitoring invoice payments and noting when a customer payment is late.

Top 10 Statements You Never Want to Hear
#3: "Don't Contact This Customer about His Late Payments"

Motivation

If you are motivated solely by profit, you will not be a good factor, you will neither deserve nor earn your clients' loyalty, and you will not enjoy the people with whom you work.
Factoring Case Studies (2nd Edition)
Assessment

If you go into factoring only to help people, your good intentions will get slaughtered and your sense of innocence shredded.
Factoring Case Studies (2nd Edition)
Assessment

Mutual Benefit

Because the factor's income is tied to the factored receivables of a client, both the factor and client increase their income as the client business grows.
Factoring: Sell Your Invoices Today, Get Cash Tomorrow
Factoring Versus Other Financing

Need for Factors

As long as businesses need cash there will always be a demand for someone to provide it. That means the necessity for prudent and prosperous small factors will be with us for a long time to come.
Fundamentals for Factors
The Past, Present, and Future of Factoring

Need for Money

Factors cannot assume a particular client will do the right thing because it is the right thing. The need for money trumps what is right just about every time.
Factoring Case Studies, 2nd edition
Dee Seetful and Associates

Niche

There are many features in a factor to look for. These features include the niche a factor serves, factoring dollar volume required, services provided, and more.

Factoring: Sell Your Invoices Today, Get Cash Tomorrow
What to Look for in a Factor

Very small businesses with low sales volume who need factoring should seek out factors who serve the niche of very small clients.

Factoring: Sell Your Invoices Today, Get Cash Tomorrow
What to Look for in a Factor

When you discuss with a factor the niche he serves, don't try to make your business conform to that niche if in fact it doesn't. You're better served to find a factor who prefers to work with a company your size or with your industry.

Factoring: Sell Your Invoices Today, Get Cash Tomorrow
What to Look for in a Factor

Notice of Assignment

The Notice of Assignment is a standard but very important document in factoring transactions. It is a letter that provides the factor with a great deal of protection if it is properly executed, and every factor should make a point of requiring this document.

Top 10 Illusions about Risk and Loss
#7: Once a Customer Receives a Notice of Assignment, Sending Payment to the Factor as Instructed Will Not Be a Problem

The NOA makes very clear that the client is in a factoring relationship, has formally assigned his receivables to the factor, and the customer is now instructed and obligated to pay the factor directly for the client's invoices. If the customer does not pay the factor, their obligations for any invoice which are not paid to the factor have not been met.

Top 10 Illusions about Risk and Loss
#7: Once a Customer Receives a Notice of Assignment, Sending Payment to the Factor as Instructed Will Not Be a Problem

Most important, the letter should say the only way this letter can be released is in writing by an officer of the factoring company.
Top 10 Illusions about Risk and Loss
#7: Once a Customer Receives a Notice of Assignment, Sending Payment to the Factor as Instructed Will Not Be a Problem

Incompetence and disorganization on the part of the customer can thwart the purpose of the NOA.
Top 10 Illusions about Risk and Loss
#7: Once a Customer Receives a Notice of Assignment, Sending Payment to the Factor as Instructed Will Not Be a Problem

While an NOA can be correctly executed at the beginning – properly delivered, properly received, properly noted by the customer's Accounts Payable department – it can take no time, a little time or quite some time for that same AP department to really mess it up.
Top 10 Illusions about Risk and Loss
#7: Once a Customer Receives a Notice of Assignment, Sending Payment to the Factor as Instructed Will Not Be a Problem

Other Financing

If you have ever applied for a bank loan, you'll find the application process with factors to be much simpler and faster.
Factoring: Sell Your Invoices Today, Get Cash Tomorrow
Signing On

If you have an immediate need for cash, waiting for loans (which must be paid back) can literally be a business killer. I can't count the number of exasperated (and often nearly desperate) small business owners who have sought factoring after experiencing nothing but frustration in applying for these programs.
Factoring: Sell Your Invoices Today, Get Cash Tomorrow
Factoring Versus Other Financing

Unless you already have experience and multiple contacts in a related cash flow business, stick to factoring and stay clear of brokering loans or venture capital.
How to Run a Small Factoring Business
Common Mistakes

Payment Over Notice

If the customer "pays over notice" (i.e. pays the client instead of the factor), the customer may legally have to make a second payment to the factor if the first payment never makes its way into the factor's hands.

Top 10 Illusions about Risk and Loss
#7: Once a Customer Receives a Notice of Assignment, Sending Payment to the Factor as Instructed Will Not Be a Problem

Despite often Herculean efforts on your part to provide a Notice of Assignment and make follow-up calls to be sure they will pay you and not the client, followed by assurances they will, guess what? Many customers *still* make their checks to your clients anyway. This leads you to wonder about the intelligence of a great many accounts payable departments across the country, as well as being one of the most effective means of rapidly turning your hair gray.

How to Run a Small Factoring Business
Banking and Funds Transfers

Despite all the steps factors take, I never cease to be amazed at how frequently payment over notice occurs. Dealing with AP departments for many years has led me to develop a kind of conspiracy theory against factors.

How to Run a Small Factoring Business
Record Keeping

Payroll

By factoring regularly, most companies have sufficient cash to meet payroll each time without a problem. Without factoring, telling employees to wait a few days to deposit their checks is an unpleasant but familiar event for some cash-strapped companies. It is *never* greeted with enthusiasm by the workers.

Top 10 Quotes on the Benefits of Factoring
#4: "My Payroll Is Met Easily Every Week, and I Have a Better Relationship with My Employees and Suppliers."

Pay When Paid

Pay when paid arrangements add extra layers of risk because you're far removed from the company for whom the work is done and pretty

powerless to do anything when slow and/or short payments happen. Clearly this is not the best scenario to factor.
How to Run a Small Factoring Business
Common Mistakes

People-Centered Business

This is a very people-centric enterprise. If individuals don't fascinate you, you probably will not find factoring very interesting. Exasperating at times – yes; quite lucrative at times – no question; but interesting…no.
Factoring Case Studies (2nd Edition)
Introduction

Factoring is primarily a people and relationships business, with some office procedures and tasks thrown in. If you are good with people, fair minded, determined to do what is helpful for others and good for your business, and have good common sense as it applies to business and finances, you'll conquer the most important parts.
Fundamentals for Factors
Is Factoring Right for You?

Factoring is an intensely people-centered business. Factoring certainly involves business financing, but it is far more than that. Factoring is relationships. Factoring requires trust while demanding street smarts. Factoring requires common sense. Factoring brings out the very best and the very worst in people.
Factoring Case Studies (2nd Edition)
Assessment

Perceptions of Factoring

A bank manager once told me his colleagues consider factors to be "the used car salesmen of the financial world." Isn't that inspiring?
How to Run a Small Factoring Business
What I've Learned about the Factoring Industry

If factoring will increase your bottom line, deciding not to factor will actually cost your company money. In the sample manufacturing company's comparison cited earlier, not factoring would have cost the business $17,000 in missed opportunities. Why would someone do

this? Probably because his accountant told him factoring was "too expensive."
Factoring: Sell Your Invoices Today, Get Cash Tomorrow
Faulty Assumptions and Mistakes to Avoid

For better or worse, factoring is one of the best-kept secrets from the general public in this country.
Factoring: Sell Your Invoices Today, Get Cash Tomorrow
Why Haven't I Heard of This Before?

Personal Guarantees

A personal guarantee states that regardless of what happens to his business, your client will personally make good on any money owed you. This gives you greater protection if his business flops, provided he has the personal resources to pay what you're owed.
How to Run a Small Factoring Business
Due Diligence

Make sure the business owner's personal resources are sufficient or a personal guarantee is worthless.
How to Run a Small Factoring Business
Due Diligence
When a problem account is given to collections, one of the first things the collection agency or attorney asks is, "Do you have a signed Personal Guarantee?"
Top 10 Illusions about Risk and Loss
#5: The Signature on Your Contract or Personal Guarantee of a Different Person than the One Receiving Advances Provides You Adequate Legal Protection

If a business owner is unwilling to sign your contract documents and wants someone else to do it on his behalf – especially the Personal Guarantee – watch out! Especially if the owner appears to be an experienced, business-savvy individual and he won't sign anything tying him to responsibility whatsoever, chances are good that you're going to regret someone else's signature on your documents.
Top 10 Illusions about Risk and Loss
#5: The Signature on Your Contract or Personal Guarantee of a Different Person than the One Receiving Advances Provides You Adequate Legal Protection

Potential of Factoring

Imagine just for a moment the effect on our nation's economy if a vast number of small and startup companies had access to all the operating capital they needed to grow. What would happen if hundreds of thousands and even millions of small companies could obtain *unlimited funds without a loan?*

Factoring: Sell Your Invoices Today, Get Cash Tomorrow
Why Haven't I Heard of This Before?

Pressure

If the prospect wants you to hurry up your procedures, beware. Don't be rushed. Take the time necessary to do the due diligence you feel is needed. If the prospect isn't willing or able to wait for this, she probably won't be the kind of client with whom you want to work.

How to Run a Small Factoring Business
Common Mistakes

Quality Investment

Is this a quality investment? Answering that question usually makes the decision to accept or decline an application quite easy. If the answer is "yes," I accept the client; if it's "no," I don't. No rocket science here.

Top 10 Insights about Factoring Prospects
#2: Is This a Quality Investment?

If you have doubts about someone being a quality investment and forge ahead anyway, you will come to know all too well the truth of the statement: "Having *no* client is better than having a *bad* client."

Top 10 Insights about Factoring Prospects
#2: Is This a Quality Investment?

Rebates

Asking when rebates are paid is a significant question. Don't just assume you'll get your full rebate back immediately, especially if the factor doesn't clearly explain how he pays rebates. You want to be very clear about when you will be paid rebates, how much, and how the amount paid is calculated.

Top 10 Questions to Ask When Looking for a Factor
#3: "What Are the Factor's Funding Methods and Rebate Practices?"

If you are unclear about the calculation method and when rebates are paid, ask and ask again until it makes sense. This is not an area where you want a fuzzy understanding, because getting your rebate in a timely manner can make a difference to your cash flow.

Top 10 Questions to Ask When Looking for a Factor
#3: "What Are the Factor's Funding Methods and Rebate Practices?"

Record Keeping

Poor record keeping makes you look unprofessional to clients, customers, and colleagues. It can cost you dearly if there are ever tax questions, or a dispute as to whether an invoice was mailed, its payment received, rebates paid, and so on.

How to Run a Small Factoring Business
Common Mistakes

The more complete, accurate and systematically filed your records are, the better for everybody.

How to Run a Small Factoring Business
Record Keeping

Recourse Factoring

If the customer isn't good for the invoice and your client can't make it good either, you still end up eating the loss. Recourse to the client is only as good as that client's ability to pay.

How to Run a Small Factoring Business
Reducing Your Risk

Referrals

Making sure people clearly understand what you do – and that you'll give them a finder's fee for leads that eventually fund – is the secret to gaining good referrals as a small factor.

Fundamentals for Factors
Identifying and Locating Prospective Clients

Referrals from Clients

As a factor, my best leads often come from my clients. I like these leads because I know the person providing the referral – my client – understands first-hand how factoring works and appreciates what factoring does for him. His contagious enthusiasm is the best sales tool I could ever hope for.

Top 10 Quotes on the Benefits of Factoring
#6: "I Have A Friend/Relative/Colleague Who Is Interested in Your Factoring Service."

Client referrals are hands down the best, cheapest, and most effective advertising you can get.

How to Run a Small Factoring Business
Marketing: How to Find Clients

Relationships

Factors deal with finances and business procedures, but everything comes down to human interactions. These relations involve reciprocal trust and working together for mutual benefit.

Factoring Case Studies (2nd Edition)
Assessment

No matter how wonderful your website, how spectacular your brochure, or how glossy your business card, the ultimate success of your business is your relationships and how you handle them.

Marketing Methods for Small Factors & Brokers
Anne Gordon

Factoring is an intensely people-centered business. Factoring certainly involves business financing, but it is far more than that. Factoring is relationships. Factoring requires trust while demanding street smarts. Factoring requires common sense. Factoring brings out the very best and the very worst in people.

Factoring Case Studies (2nd Edition)
Assessment

Rewards

Yes, factoring can be risky. Factoring can also be extremely rewarding when you work with good people, know you are providing a much-needed service, follow sound business practices, and make a very high return on investment.

Factoring Case Studies (2nd Edition)
Assessment

Right Reasons to Factor

When factoring is used for the proper job – stabilizing cash flow, company growth and expansion – you will be amazed at how well it can work.

Factoring: Sell Your Invoices Today, Get Cash Tomorrow
Faulty Assumptions and Mistakes to Avoid

If selling your receivables will increase your volume of business by increasing production capability and/or creating more sales, you are probably using factoring for the right reasons.

Factoring: Sell Your Invoices Today, Get Cash Tomorrow
Faulty Assumptions and Mistakes to Avoid

Risk

If you are highly risk-averse, factoring is not for you.

Factoring Case Studies (2nd Edition)
Assessment

Factors sooner or later can lose money from some (and if you do it long enough, all) of the following risks:
1. Nonpayment from customers.
2. Poor management of client businesses.
3. Personal events, usually in the lives of clients, that adversely affect their operation.
4. Fraud.

Fundamentals for Factors
Factoring Risks

Numerous risks go with factoring – dishonest, selfish, careless, and otherwise untrustworthy clients and customers, and errors in procedures or judgment made by factors. Therefore common sense suggests a factor's foremost strategy is to set financial limits, thereby putting minimal amounts at risk. This is especially prudent when the factor is new, even if his or her pool of factoring funds is sizeable.

Factoring Case Studies (2nd Edition)
Assessment

While long-term clients are the best to have, they're still not completely risk-free. There is no such thing in the factoring business. Live with it. If you can't, don't go into the business in the first place.

Top 10 Illusions about Risk and Loss
#1: There Is Little or No Risk Posed By a Client Who Has Factored with You for Years

Continue to maintain low exposures, never to let your guard down, and never to assume your procedures make you invincible. Factoring involves risk; therefore you must follow specific strategies to minimize your risk at all times.

Factoring Case Studies, 2nd edition
Assessment

By its very nature, factoring is a risky business. You're handing money over to another person who owns a business, and despite all the contracts and personal guarantees and invoice verifications and follow up calls and legal and collection actions you take, you are simply never, ever absolutely 100% certain that your money will return to you.

Top 10 Illusions about Risk and Loss
#1: There Is Little or No Risk Posed By a Client Who Has Factored with You for Years

The factoring landscape is littered with land mines, and risks lurk under even the most innocent-looking stones. Factors are constantly vulnerable to client dishonesty, poor management, customer ineptitude, and the unexpected "stuff" that ordinary life includes. Add to this many common mistakes factors can make without realizing it, and you can see why factors earn the higher rates they do: it's a matter of compensating for the risks they take every day.

Factoring Case Studies, 2nd edition
Assessment

Risk Management

While factoring is not for the faint of heart, neither is it for the reckless.

How to Run a Small Factoring Business
Money

The players who are most successful in the long run are the most patient, careful and methodical – not the highest rollers.
How to Run a Small Factoring Business
Money

One might look upon investing in business receivables as a well calculated gamble, which managed properly, leans the odds of winning heavily in your favor.
Fundamentals for Factors
Risk Management Tools

The safeguards you can put in place fall into four general categories:
1. Set financial limits
2. Determine industries you will and will not factor.
3. Perform adequate due diligence.
4. Establish and build up reserves.

Fundamentals for Factors
Risk Management Tools

You must structure your operation so that a catastrophic loss can't happen, and any losses you do experience are small enough to absorb.
Fundamentals for Factors
Factoring Risks

Spread your money around in small enough piles that if you lose any one or even two of them, the rest will keep you going and you will hardly feel a ripple.
How to Run a Small Factoring Business
Bits of Wisdom for the Small Factor

Without question, avoiding over concentrations is by far the most important safeguard you can implement. If you religiously follow all other risk management practices but overlook this one, you can still lose big time and be out of business in a heartbeat.
How to Run a Small Factoring Business
Reducing Your Risk

Services

While factoring is a business whose focus is financing, it is especially a service business. Factors provide their clients numerous services.
Factoring: Sell Your Invoices Today, Get Cash Tomorrow
What to Look for in a Factor

Slow Payments

Because slower customer payments result in increased discounts the client pays (and the factor receives), many people assume there is little incentive for factors to desire or encourage fast payments from customers. They reason that factors will have little interest in urging prompt customer payment. This is quite erroneous.
Factoring: Sell Your Invoices Today, Get Cash Tomorrow
Faulty Assumptions and Mistakes to Avoid

There is simply no good reason you shouldn't inquire about a slow-paying invoice, particularly if your follow up calls are done in a professional manner. Any time a client is nervous about your contact with a customer, or tells you not to contact a customer about a late payment, you should see the proverbial red flag hoisted and flapping wildly in the wind. With four spotlights beaming on it. And booming fireworks. And a big brass band blasting a John Philip Sousa march. *Notice* it, already.
Top 10 Statements You Never Want to Hear
#3: "Don't Contact This Customer about His Late Payments"

When presented with a federal government invoice that will (maybe) take 60 or (possibly) 90 or (could be) 120 days to pay – or a client's invoice to a steady customer that I know will pay in 30 days, I'll take the good 30 day invoice any day.
Top 10 Insights about Factoring Prospects
#6: Give Me a Good 30-Day Invoice Any Day

Don't let slow payments get too far out there.
Top 10 Statements You Never Want to Hear
#4: "Don't Worry...You'll Get Your Money Back"

Don't factor accounts that take too long to pay (they tie up your money and may never pay).
How to Run a Small Factoring Business
Money

Spot Factoring

I don't do spot factoring so I have no "one-timers" which I consider a waste of time, considering the effort it takes to set up an account before you earn income from it. Having only one payout from a spot factoring deal has never seemed worth the effort to me as a factor of small clients.
How I Run My One-Person Factoring Business
My Clients

Success

Success can be measured by a wide variety of yardsticks. We might divide the benchmarks for success into three broad categories:
1. Success measured by numbers
2. Success measured by client business advancement
3. Success measured by personal satisfaction
Fundamentals for Factors
Measuring Success & Determining What It Takes

For those who wish to factor successfully, they must find a middle ground where sound business practices, prudence and common sense overcome greed or excessive generosity.
Fundamentals for Factors
Factoring Risks

If you factor with a realistic approach, a cautious attitude, and a desire to improve your clients' lives as well as your own, you will find factoring a fascinating and highly rewarding business.
Factoring Case Studies (2nd Edition)
Assessment

Factors who run their operations properly, show sound judgment, use common sense, make excellent income, and help many businesses, tend to stick around.

Factoring Case Studies (2nd Edition)
Assessment

Telling Your Customers

A common concern among many business owners who consider factoring their receivables is their customers' reaction. They might worry, "Will they think I'm in financial trouble?" "Will they stop doing business with me?" "Will they refuse to pay a factor?" While these concerns are not uncommon, the vast majority of the time they are quite groundless, as is soon discovered.

Factoring: Sell Your Invoices Today, Get Cash Tomorrow
Telling Your Customers

When a company factors its receivables, "what their customers think" about their financial stability is simply and completely irrelevant. The truth is, they just don't think about it at all.

Top 10 Misconceptions about Factoring
#1: "When a Company Factors, Customers Will Think It's in Financial Trouble"

You are outsourcing your receivables management, just like many companies outsource their payroll management. Doing so is giving you improved cash flow and frees you from a time-consuming task that is not profitable for your business. By outsourcing this job, you're now able to provide an even better product or service.

Factoring: Sell Your Invoices Today, Get Cash Tomorrow
Telling Your Customers

Trust

Factors deal with finances and business procedures, but everything comes down to human interactions. These relations involve reciprocal trust and working together for mutual benefit.

Factoring Case Studies (2nd Edition)
Assessment

If your only purpose in factoring is the money you make, your clients will sense this quickly or eventually learn it, and their trust in you will become shrouded.
How to Run a Small Factoring Business
What I've Learned about the Factoring Industry

Your client must trust you as she would her banker, accountant, lawyer, doctor, pastor, rabbi, and anyone else in whom she entrusts the welfare of her life and business.
How to Run a Small Factoring Business
Reducing Your Risk

Verifications

Invoice verifications often act as a quality control device. If your customer has as issue or dispute over an invoice, this can come to light during verification. Thus you solve the problem immediately, keep your customer happy, and obtain immediate cash at the same time.
Factoring: Sell Your Invoices Today, Get Cash Tomorrow
Factoring Procedures

The more you verify invoices the safer you'll be.
How to Run a Small Factoring Business
Record Keeping

Verify invoices to make sure the product or service has been received and payment will be made to the factor's address. Many of the bad experiences resulted because the factors neglected these verifications.
Factoring Case Studies (2nd Edition)
Assessment

I had one temp agency client forge every time card she submitted for months and I didn't verify them; I just assumed the time card signatures were legitimate. It was only when the invoices weren't paid that I called the customers. Incredibly, they had never heard of her or her company. If I had verified only a handful of these at the beginning, I would have avoided a lot of problems.
How to Run a Small Factoring Business
Record Keeping

Being "consistent in your inconsistency" is a good practice for verifications. That is, if you have an unpredictable pattern to your verification practices, a dishonest client will have a harder time getting away with fraudulent invoices and/or phony customer approvals.

How to Run a Small Factoring Business
Record Keeping

Virtual Office

With the wonders of today's technology, running a virtual company is not only possible, it's easy.

How I Run My Virtual Factoring Office
What Is a Virtual Office?

Several years ago when I began my factoring business, I knew I wanted to work from home. I had my fill of a daily commute, nearby co-workers' radios droning annoyingly all day, and little control over my work environment. I didn't know it at the time, but I wanted to work in a virtual office.

How I Run My Virtual Factoring Office
What Is a Virtual Office?

I like working from home. I like wearing comfortable and very casual clothes every day. I like spending zero time commuting daily. I like having my dog by my side all day. For me, small is good and bigger is not necessarily better.

How I Run My Virtual Factoring Office
My Virtual Office

Who needs a big fancy office with dozens of employees in a single location to be happy? Not me. I'll work in my frumpy clothes at my virtual office with a snoring dog at my feet, any time.

How I Run My Virtual Factoring Office
My Virtual Office

Warning Signs

Any time a bill is late being paid, especially from a dependable customer, and the client does not appear concerned about the delay (which means they're paying you more), something is wrong.

Factoring Case Studies, 2nd edition
Dee Seetful and Associates

You Can't Help Everyone

If a prospect does not fit into the parameters of factoring, don't lead him on. As difficult as it may be sometimes, tell the truth, and do it sooner rather than later. Both of you will be better for it.

Marketing Methods for Small Factors & Brokers
Anne Gordon

Sooner or later (probably sooner) you're going to realize you just can't help everyone; not because you don't have enough capital, but because many of the prospects you meet can't (or shouldn't) be factored.

- Some don't have factorable invoices.
- Some don't have a factorable company.
- Some will be ineligible due to personal history or financial circumstances.
- Some need to get out of business or shouldn't be in business in the first place.

Top 10 Insights about Factoring Prospects
#9: You Can't Help Everyone

Books and Ebooks Referenced

The Small Factor Series

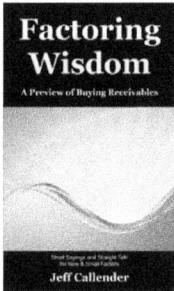

Book 1
Factoring Wisdom:
A Preview of
Buying Receivables

Short Sayings and Straight Talk
For New & Small Factors

Book 2
Fundamentals
for Factors

How You Can Make
Large Returns in Small Receivables

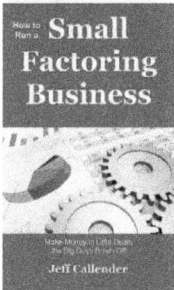

Book 3
How to Run
a Small Factoring Business

Make Money in Little Deals
the Big Guys Brush Off

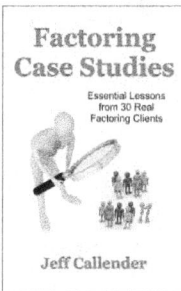

Book 4
Factoring Case Studies
(2nd Edition)

Essential Lessons from
30 Real Factoring Clients

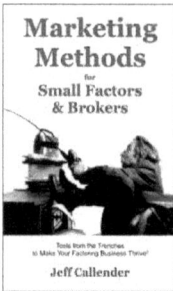

Book 5
Marketing Methods
for Small Factors
and Brokers

Tools from the Trenches
To Make Your Factoring Business Thrive!

About This Series

The Small Factor Series is designed to:

1. Provide a succinct introduction and summary of the books in this series as well as other writings by Jeff Callender.

2. Introduce readers to the investment of factoring small business receivables.

3. Provide a step-by-step manual with complete instructions for small factors.

4. Provide 30 real-life examples of factoring clients from the files of people who have been investing in small receivables for some time.

5. Describe and analyze numerous marketing methods to bring in new business which have been used by the eight contributors to the book.

Each book in the series is written to address the above points:

- Book 1, *Factoring Wisdom: A Preview of Buying Receivables,* introduces and summarizes the other books with brief excerpts from each, and arranges them by subject matter.

- Book 2, *Fundamentals for Factors* introduces potential factors to the business.

- Book 3, *How to Run a Small Factoring Business,* is the step-by-step manual.

- Book 4, *Factoring Case Studies* (2nd Edition), describes experiences of 30 real clients of small factors, which illustrate the many lessons and suggestions made in Books 2 and 3.

- Book 5, *Marketing Methods for Small Factors & Brokers*, includes contributions from seven small factors and an experienced broker.

Other Books by Jeff Callender

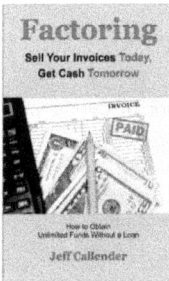

Factoring:
Sell Your Invoices Today,
Get Cash Tomorrow

How to Obtain Unlimited Funds without a Loan

Written to introduce factoring to small business owners, this book compares factoring to traditional lending, shows how it can help a company's cash flow, and guides readers in determining if factoring can improve their business.

The above books are available in the following formats from DashPointPublishing.com:

- Paperback
- PDF
- Kindle
- iPad & Android (ePub)

Ebooks by Jeff Callender

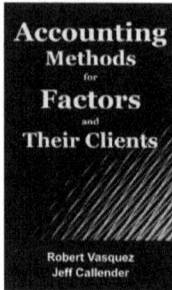

Accounting Methods for Factors and Their Clients

By Robert Vasquez and Jeff Callender

This ebook describes how to establish and maintain proper bookkeeping records for a factoring company and factoring clients. You'll learn how to use GAAP-approved procedures and make sure you're doing it right. Following these step-by-step instructions starts you on the right foot.

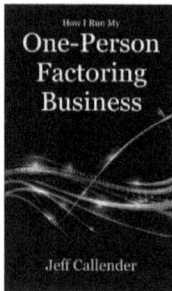

How I Run My One-Person Factoring Business

Want to get started running a small factoring business by yourself? This ebook shows how the author successfully began as a one-person operation, and the everyday tools you can use now to do the same.

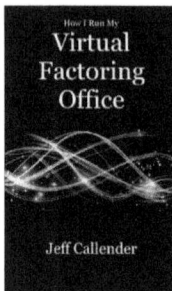

How I Run My Virtual Factoring Office

A virtual office means you can work from just about anywhere you want. Learn the common tools and technology the author uses (available to anyone) to run his virtual factoring office. Enjoy the comforts of home – at work!

"Top 10" Ebooks by Jeff Callender
"Top 10" Ebooks for Factors:

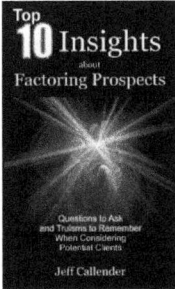

Top 10 Insights
about Factoring Prospects

Questions to Ask
and Truisms to Remember
When Considering Potential Clients

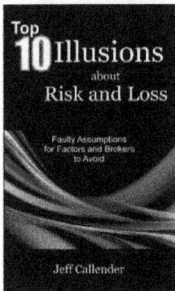

Top 10 Illusions
about Risk and Loss

Faulty Assumptions for
Factors and Brokers to Avoid

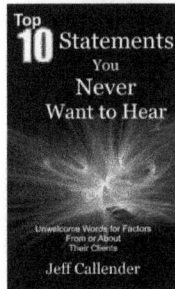

Top 10 Statements
You Never Want to Hear

Unwelcome Words for Factors
From or About Their Clients

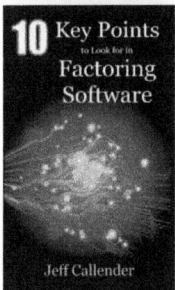

10 Key Points to Look for
in Factoring Software

Consider these 10 issues
before purchasing software
for your factoring operation

"Top 10" Ebooks for Clients:

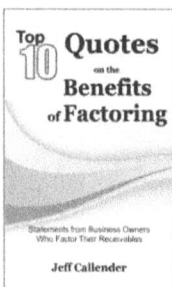

Top 10 Quotes on the Benefits of Factoring

Statements from Business Owners
Who Factor Their Receivables

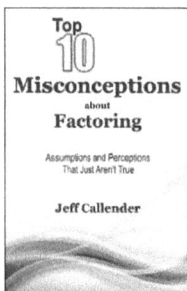

Top 10 Misconceptions about Factoring

Assumptions and Perceptions
That Just Aren't True

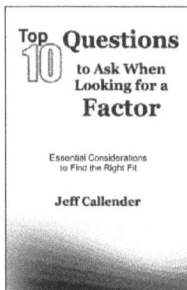

Top 10 Questions to Ask When Looking for a Factor

Essential Considerations
to Find the Right Fit

The above ebooks are available in the following formats from DashPointPublishing.com:

- PDF
- Kindle
- iPad & Android

Acknowledgements

I would like to thank the following people for the important parts they played in creating this book:

Nicole Jones for her proofreading skills and creating the ebook versions of books in the Small Factor Series and all other titles, and making them available to the world.

Anne Gordon for her proofreading skills and valuable experience, comments, suggestions, and support.

Cover image credit: © Sylenko Svetlana/123RF.com.

Important Notice

This publication is for educational purposes only and is not intended to give legal, tax, or professional advice. If such service is needed, the reader should seek professional advice from a competent attorney or accountant.

The author assumes no responsibility for any financial losses a reader may experience as a result of any factoring or other business transaction.

Also by Jeff Callender

Paperbacks and Ebooks
The Small Factor Series includes 5 titles:

1. *Factoring Wisdom: A Preview of Buying Receivables*
   Short Sayings and Straight Talk for New & Small Factors © 2012
2. *Fundamentals for Factors*
   How You Can Make Large Returns in Small Receivables © 2012
3. *How to Run a Small Factoring Business*
   Make Money in Little Deals the Big Guys Brush Off © 2012
4. *Factoring Case Studies*
   Essential Lessons from 30 Real Factoring Clients
   1st edition ©2003, 2005; 2nd edition © 2012
5. *Marketing Methods for Small Factors & Brokers*
   Tools from the Trenches to Make Your Factoring Business Thrive!
   © 2012

Factoring: Sell Your Invoices Today, Get Cash Tomorrow
   How to Obtain Unlimited Funds without a Loan © 2012

eBooks
For Factoring Clients:
Accounting Methods for Factors & Their Clients © 2012
Top 10 Quotes on the Benefits of Factoring © 2012
Top 10 Misconceptions about Factoring © 2012
Top 10 Questions to Ask When Looking for a Factor © 2012

For Factors:
Accounting Methods for Factors & Their Clients © 2012
How I Run My One-Person Factoring Business © 2008, 2012
How I Run My Virtual Factoring Office © 2012
Top 10 Insights about Factoring Prospects © 2008, 2012
Top 10 Illusions about Risk and Loss © 2008, 2012
Top 10 Statements You Never Want to Hear © 2008, 2012
10 Key Points to Look for in Factoring Software © 2008, 2012

Spreadsheet Calculators
APR and Income Calculators © 2002, 2012

Software
FactorFox Software © 2006 – current year

Websites
www.DashPointPublishing.com   www.SmallFactor.com
www.DashPointFinancial.com   www.SmallFactorAcademy.com
www.FactorFox.com   www.FactorFind.com

About the Author

Jeff Callender had an unusual start to his business career. Though he is the son and grandson of businessmen, he began his working life as a pastor.

After earning a college degree in Sociology and a Master of Divinity degree, he served three churches in Washington state over 14 years. While he found ministry rewarding, he realized he had an entrepreneurial spirit which gradually pulled him toward business.

He left his career in the church and about a year later stumbled onto factoring. He began as a broker but after numerous referrals were declined only because of their small size, he started factoring very small clients himself. His career as a factor – and as a pioneer in the niche of very small receivables factoring – was thus born in 1994.

He has worked with a great number of very small business owners in need of factoring. He wrote his first book, *Factoring Small Receivables*, in 1995, and since then has written numerous books, ebooks, and articles, and spoken at many events in the factoring industry. His writing and two decades of experience have established him as a leading authority in the niche of small business factoring.

Jeff is the President of three companies he started. Dash Point Financial provides factoring services to small business owners throughout the U.S. It also provides the nucleus of his experience for writing. Learn more at DashPointFinancial.com.

Dash Point Publishing publishes and sells his books and ebooks, as well as those of other authors who write about factoring. His paperbacks are available from DashPointPublishing.com, as well as Amazon, the Kindle bookstore, Apple's iBookstore, and other online ebook sellers. Dash Point Publishing's website provides additional materials such as legal documents for smaller factoring companies.

FactorFox Software offers a cloud-based database solution for factors to track their client transactions. Originally based on his own company's back-office operational needs, readers of his books will feel right at home using the software in their own factoring companies. It has become one of the top platforms for the industry and is used by factoring companies throughout the world. More information can be found at FactorFox.com.

Having grown up in southern California, Jeff now lives in Tacoma, Washington with his wife, dog, and two cats. He has a grown son and daughter.

www.ingramcontent.com/pod-product-compliance
Lightning Source LLC
Chambersburg PA
CBHW060623200326
41521CB00007B/867